JFK JR., GEORGE, & ME

JFK JR., GEORGE, & ME

MATT BERMAN

A MEMOIR

GALLERY BOOKS

NEW YORK   LONDON   TORONTO   SYDNEY   NEW DELHI

Certain names and identifying characteristics have been changed.

Gallery Books
A Division of Simon & Schuster, Inc.
1230 Avenue of the Americas
New York, NY 10020

First Gallery Books hardcover edition May 2014

GALLERY BOOKS and colophon are registered trademarks of Simon & Schuster, Inc.

For information about special discounts for bulk purchases, please contact Simon & Schuster Special Sales at 1-866-506-1949 or business@simonandschuster.com.

The Simon & Schuster Speakers Bureau can bring authors to your live event. For more information or to book an event contact the Simon & Schuster Speakers Bureau at 1-866-248-3049 or visit our website at www.simonspeakers.com.

Designed by Ben Wiseman

Manufactured in the United States of America

10 9 8 7 6 5 4 3 2 1

Library of Congress Cataloging-in-Publication Data
    Berman, Matt–
    JFK Jr., George, & me : a memoir / Matt Berman.
        pages cm
        1. Kennedy, John F. Jr., 1960–1999. 2. Kennedy, John F. Jr., 1960–1999—
Friends and associates. 3. Children of presidents—United States—Biography.
4. Celebrities—United States—Biography. 5. Berman, Matt. 1964– 6. George
(New York, N.Y.) I. Title. II: JFK Jr., George, and me.
        E843.K42B47   2014
        973.922092—dc23
        [B]   2013033582

ISBN 978-1-4516-9701-8
ISBN 978-1-4516-9727-8 (ebook)

For my mom and dad

CONTENTS

JFK JR., GEORGE, & ME

INTRODUCTION:

THROW *ME* INTO THE LION'S DEN

"Quick, come to my office. I've got Barbra on the phone, and she's not getting the idea. Talk to her and tell her how *beautiful* she's going to look dressed as Betsy Ross!"

"Oh, thanks. Throw *me* into the lion's den," I whined as John pulled me by the sleeve into his office. We had decided to try and convince Barbra Streisand to appear on the cover of *George* magazine as the mother of the American flag. But I thought I'd be working with an agent or an assistant, not Barbra herself. I nervously took the receiver from John, "Hi, I'm Matt, John's creative director."

"NAT?" the familiar voice responded.

"No, no," I corrected her. "MATT, with an *M*!"

"Oh!" she replied, "I'm Barbra with a *B*!" sounding more like Fanny Brice in *Funny Girl*.

I told her that Betsy Ross would be a great character for her, how we'd execute it perfectly. Then I suggested a photographer to take the photos. She agreed and said it would be easier to shoot at her house in Malibu than at a studio. As I was talking to her, I couldn't wait to call my uncle Morty, who loved her music so much that when I'd roll my eyes at the mention of her name, he'd stop me and say, "Easy, Matthew, you're talking about my girlfriend."

Up until this point, I'd dealt with all the cover shoots on my own, and Cindy Crawford and Robert De Niro had been big successes. But this one seemed like it would be more of a challenge. Carolyn had warned us that word on the street was that Barbra was a handful, so John decided that he'd better attend this photo shoot and lend his star power. Always trusting Carolyn's advice, I was relieved when John said he wanted to come. Three weeks later John asked me, "Maestro, what time are we flying out?" He'd nicknamed me The Maestro; I think it was because he felt so out of his element in the art department, the place I felt most comfortable.

"Friday, the noon flight on American, so we have time to figure out the Saturday shoot," I answered. Then I asked him, "Meet you at the gate?"

"Pick me up at my place and we'll go to the airport together."

I swung by his apartment at 20 North Moore, rang the buzzer, and John's voice crackled through the intercom. "Matt, I'm not ready yet, why don't you come up?" The elevator opened and I entered the loft; music by The Cardigans played in another room. His bags were lined up next to the door: a sporty tennis bag with a racket sticking out, a hanging garment bag, and a leather and canvas overnight bag. Effegenio, John's house guy, was sautéing an omelet, and John was sitting at the table in front of the biggest breakfast array imaginable; coffee, orange juice, grapefruit juice, yogurt, sliced melon, boxes of cereal, muffins, and all sorts of bagels and breads. "Matt, we've got plenty of time, sit with me and eat something."

As I was sipping my coffee, Carolyn sauntered out of the bedroom wearing gray sweatpants and a wifebeater, mussing her beautiful long, white-blonde hair. "Hey, honey," she said, drowsily pouring herself a cup of coffee. She affectionately touched the back of my neck and sat down next to me, asking, "Are you ready?" I smirked and looked up toward the ceiling, shrugging my shoulders. "Look," she said, pulling apart a bagel, "just remember what I told you at the office—make sure that whatever you say to her you say like you mean it, or she'll eat you alive." I had a few bites of raisin bread but was too wound up to eat. We were running late; I was sure we'd miss the twelve o'clock flight.

John kissed Carolyn good-bye and threw his bags into the trunk of the town car waiting downstairs. As the driver headed uptown, John pulled himself forward by the back of the driver's velour seat and asked, "Which way are you going?"

"I'm going to the Midtown Tunnel," the driver said, keeping his eyes on the road.

"I've done this trip a lot. We're better off going *downtown,* around The Battery, and taking the Williamsburg Bridge," John told him. The driver seemed annoyed, but he followed John's route. As we drove under the sign that read "Welcome to John F. Kennedy International Airport," John commented on the shabby and neglected condition of the airport: "This place is a mess."

At the American Airlines desk, the ticket agent greeted us and asked for our IDs. When he read John's driver's license, he looked up at us and started stuttering. "M-Mr. K-K-Kennedy, would you like to be s-seated t-together?" I had booked a business-class seat for myself, and John had a first-class seat. Without discussion, John put his Amex card down and said, "Yes, seat us together."

Once we settled into our seats, John fumbled with the personal video machines as if he was seeing them for the first time. "Oh, I get it, you pull it out from down here." I think it was an effort to initiate me painlessly into first-class travel.

A harried stewardess adjusted her American Airlines scarf, smoothed her hair, and made a beeline for John. "Mr. Kennedy, I just have to say, I spent last weekend with my mother and my aunt and they said, 'Why haven't you met Mr. Right yet?' and I said, 'Because I haven't met John Kennedy Jr. yet, and now I have!'" Realizing that she was ignoring the ordinary mortal seated beside John, she looked down at me with wide eyes and said,

"Hello." John, always polite, said, "Thank you, that's nice, thank you very much."

As the plane taxied to the runway I wondered what I would talk to John about for six hours. The plane lifted its wheels from the tarmac, and we soared above the clouds and leveled off. I broke the silence with small talk about the upcoming auction of Jackie Kennedy's belongings. "What kind of stuff are you keeping? Don't you want some paintings for your loft, like a Warhol or something?"

"I don't know," John said. "A lot of it's not really my taste. I kind of want to buy my own things." Changing the subject, he asked me, "What's going on with your apartment hunt, Maestro?"

"I looked at a loft with old wooden beams on the ceilings on West Street near you. The only problem is that all of the windows face the West Side Highway," I said.

"That's a lot to look at every single day," he warned me.

"And not to mention the carbon monoxide!" I added. Chatting with John was easy, and I learned not to stress about conversational topics. We were served lunch and he nodded off for most of the flight, his head propped up against the airplane window, drooling in the sunlight.

At the LAX gate, an uptight, all-business American Airlines ground control lady boarded the plane and knelt down next to our seats. "Mr. Kennedy, your rental car is waiting at the curb. There's a bit of a *scene* at the gate." We walked through the jetway into the terminal to find two dozen paparazzi waiting. Flashbulbs popping, they began shouting, "Hey, John, how's the magazine going?" "John, what are you doing in L.A.?" "John, over here," "John, where's Carolyn?" Someone had tipped them off that he was on the flight; John suspected that it was Funny Girl herself.

I was freaked out; I'd never seen anything like *this* before. It was overwhelming. "Jesus! Where should I go?" I asked him. Stepping onto the moving sidewalk, John told me to find the rental car and he'd meet me at the curb. He kept his eyes on his shoes the entire time, determined not to give anyone a decent photo. I got to the car first and waited for him to make his way through the throngs of photographers. We threw our bags into the trunk, and John drove off. As he merged into L.A. traffic, he turned to me and said, "Well, Matt, you're not going to believe this, but I think John Kennedy just arrived in L.A. with his new gay lover."

We checked in at Shutters, a beachfront hotel in Santa Monica, and John went to get some exercise. I hit the minibar and the bed. After I napped for about twenty minutes my phone rang. "Matt, what's going on?" It was my partner in crime from the office, John's right hand, RoseMarie. "How was the flight, everything okay?" She was digging for gossip. "Anything *weird* happen?" she added, prying further. John must have called her and had a laugh at my expense. Then she came clean. "Okay, John just called me from his room and said, 'Rosie, you've got to call Matt

Berman. He's on the ceiling in his room. It was a real fuck-fest of reporters at the airport.'"

He was right; it had been a full-on assault. I think John was embarrassed that I'd seen *that* side of his life. I'd worked for months with him in private locations, restaurants, his apartment, or the office, but this was the first time I'd seen what his public life could be like. In one day, I saw the extremes of John's world, and I was beginning to sense how he must have felt, constantly struggling to distinguish between intimate relationships and public ones.

1.

I HAVE ALL FOUR, YOU ONLY HAVE TWO!

I first met John in 1994. I had been working at *Elle* magazine on Madison Avenue for four years. The French publisher Hachette owned *Elle,* and I'd gotten the job by cold-calling the art department, trying to sound blasé but determined to work there. A girl with a singsong Parisian accent answered the phone, "Hello, may I *help* you?" She turned out to be the art director, Olivia Badrutt, and invited me to come in and meet everyone. I started working for her that day.

Elle was run by a group of French businessmen led by a dashing CEO named Daniel Filipacchi. Daniel would rush through the offices wearing a pair of solid gold Cartier glasses and leather-and-fabric loafers with the exact same fabric made into a matching tie. He looked like a movie producer, a French Bob Evans, and acted as if he had exactly two minutes to sign a seven-figure deal. Daniel had come to New York with two other Frenchmen, named Régis Pagniez and Jean-Louis Ginibre, to launch the French soft porn magazine *Oui,* which was giving *Penthouse* a run for its money. *Oui* showed full frontal nudity, but it was art directed with a lot of style, more like a European fashion magazine than typical porn mags.

The guys were about the same age as my dad, but Dad and his friends were nothing like this. While my dad's wild weeknights were about playing racquetball with Bill Greenbaum and picking up Chinese takeout on his way home, these guys went out late at night to jazz clubs and hot spots like Raoul's, Nell's, and Le Zinc. They came to work in limousines, took three-hour lunches, and flew to Paris on the Concorde.

Régis, the publication director, knew everything about art and food and film. He had the most refined taste of anyone I've ever known. His daily uniform was a Brooks Brothers blue blazer, pale blue oxford shirt, gray flannel pants, and Hermès shoes. I liked the idea of having a uniform and invented a junior version of my own, wearing Levi's, a navy agnès b. zip-up sweatshirt, and Paraboot shoes. Régis was a legendary art director. I stood beside him assisting in any way I could, pouring his Coke into a glass (he would never drink from the can) and Xeroxing a word in ten different sizes so he could select and place the perfectly proportioned headline next to the perfectly cropped photograph.

The editorial staff of *Elle* was largely from the upper crust of Parisian society. Everyone's father or husband or brother was somebody well known in Paris. The fashion editor who dressed the models for the covers was the daughter of Jean Louis David, the Vidal Sassoon of France. The food editor was the wife of Jean-Pierre Cassel, the famous French movie star, and the mother of the actor Vincent Cassel, who as a teenager used to hang out at the office and help his mother on shoots. On the business side, there were people who had fathers, uncles, or friends in the French government. My laid-back Brazilian intern was well connected among the senior executives and wasn't exactly worried about job security. She took thirty-five minutes to do a round-trip job at the copy machine, slowly sauntering down the hallway like she was strolling along Ipanema beach without a care in the world. There were several attractive women at the office who held less important positions, like editing the astrology page or the travel stories, and I always wondered what credentials they had. Later, I learned that some of them were former Air France stewardesses who, I imagined, had been hired at thirty thousand feet by the Hachette playboys.

I took note of what my French bosses ordered in restaurants, and I listened to what they said about how people should behave. I tried to understand what they considered chic, which was always understated. It was the industry's best graduate program in style, and I was getting paid for it. When it was my turn to order at a restaurant, I followed the rules I'd learned and never ordered a beef carpaccio appetizer and a poached salmon entrée; meat and fish were never mixed. When white wine was poured, I'd hold my glass by the stem to be sure my hand didn't warm the chilled Sancerre; when red was on the table, I held my glass however I liked.

The subject of food and weight triggered lots of reactions. I was at a staff lunch at Café Un Deux Trois on West Forty-fourth Street, and a waiter asked me, "Would you like fries with that?" I heard Sabine Cassel *tsk-tsk*ing from the other end of the table, "*Oh là là, il est trop jeune pour être si gros.*" (He is too young to be so fat.) I realized five pounds overweight meant fat in France. I once asked another editor how I could knock off a few pounds and she said, "Matt, have you seen pictures of those people in Auschwitz?" I nodded, acting cool, though I was horrified at where she was headed with this. "Did they look fat, Matt?" I shook my head from side to side. "Do you know why? Because they *didn't eat*."

What mattered at *Elle* was beauty, and there was plenty to learn about that. I was standing next to Régis looking at the December 1988 cover of supermodel Yasmin Parvaneh (later Le Bon). It was a photo of her head and neck, the background blurred. She wore a black turtleneck, small gold hoop earrings, with her hair pulled back in a tight bun. "It's *so* boring," I said. Régis replied, "Matt, this cover is good, because this girl is the perfect *age*." I was learning a new language. I couldn't *speak* it yet, but I was starting to *hear* it.

Things at *Elle* were scrutinized in a way I hadn't imagined. From the width of a typeface, to the length of a skirt, everything was *judged*. I once bought a chartreuse shirt to try to break out of my safe navy blue sweatshirt routine. Olivia shook her head from side to side and said, "Oh là là, Matt, you are too white to wear this color." Seeing my crestfallen face, she said, "Well, maybe if you get a tan." Régis added, "Or if you were black." I wore navy the next day.

Elle didn't look like anything else on the newsstand, with its crisp Swiss design and in-your-face photos. It had a bold point of view in its photography, as well as in its styling, mixing clothes in a way Americans weren't used to. We did profiles on Régis's fashion designer friends Azzedine Alaïa, Jean Paul Gaultier, and Claude Montana. They would come into the office to drink red wine, admire our postcard view of midtown, and watch us lay out the magazine.

Years later, while I was living in Paris, I sat next to Claude Montana at a café, Le Nemours, at Palais-Royal. There was no mistaking him, with his fried and dyed orange hair, bright blue quilted leather bolero jacket, skintight red leather pants, and motorcycle boots. He was by himself, eating a parfait glass full of fromage blanc and sipping white wine. Seeing him, I was transported back to 1988 faster than hearing George Michael's *Faith*. I took a gulp of wine for courage and leaned toward him, reminding him who I was. He was a little tipsy, but he was kind to me and chatted for half an hour about his childhood with his strict father, his rise to fashion superstardom, and his fall from grace. It was sad to see him there, all alone, dressed in his outfit, and it made me miss the madness of the '80s, when there *were* people like him to inspire us.

Along with fashion, we did profiles on Régis's artist friends Red Grooms, César Baldaccini, and David Hockney, as well as layout interviews with stars Winona Ryder, Johnny Depp, and the B-52s. While we were shooting the B-52s, one of our Parisian stylists handed Kate Pierson a dress to wear for the picture. Kate held the dress in front of her by its straps and in her precise Southern accent declined, saying, "It's *aw-fully* conservative."

I'd been close to famous people before, on the street or in restaurants, but for the first time I was in a professional environment interacting with celebrities. To see them doing mundane things like asking where the bathroom was or making a personal phone call fascinated me. Were they just like everyone else? To test the waters, I walked up to Fred Schneider, who was eating a plate of pasta salad, and asked, "How's the food?" "Not bad," he answered while chewing. To me it felt like magic. They *were* real.

In the '70s, nostalgia for the golden age of Hollywood, especially the 1930s and '40s, had been everywhere. *The Sting, Paper Moon,* and *Chinatown* were huge hits, there were Marlene Dietrich film festivals at Radio City Music Hall, towels at Bloomingdale's had Garbo's face printed on them, plaster statuettes of W. C. Fields stood in every card shop, and Andy Warhol was featuring Rita Hayworth in *Interview* magazine. When we were ten or eleven, my cousin Adam and I went to see the movie *That's Entertainment!* and we became obsessed seeing all the dried-up old movie stars commenting on the spectacular movie clips. I bought a book advertised in the back of the magazine *Rona Barrett's Hollywood* called *The Movie Star Address Book,* and Adam and I sent out letters to stars asking for autographed pictures. It became a competition, and we'd compare notes week to week. I'd phone Adam: "I got one from Bob Hope today." "I did too," Adam responded, stealing my thunder. "Mine says, '*To Matt,* Best*, Bob Hope.*'" Adam, with an evil chuckle, answered, "Well, *mine* says, '*To Adam,* Sincerely, *Bob Hope.*'" We'd compare our collections of photos, marveling that these famous people had taken the time to sign a photo and mail it to us; they seemed galaxies away from our lives in Stamford. I shut Adam down for good the day I received an envelope with the return address of 70 North Rossmore Avenue, Los Angeles, CA. I opened the manila envelope and pulled out a glossy photo that read *To Matt, Sin-cerely, Mae West,* in orange marker.

At *Elle* there were often famous people in the office. Each day at around 1:00 p.m., I'd look up from my work to see who was coming in to meet Régis for lunch. Frequently, it was one of the cover models, like Elle Macpherson or Ashley Richardson or Rachel Williams, who entered the art room like graceful giraffes. My favorite guest was the Trinidadian actor Geoffrey Holder. Holder was a longtime pal of Régis and his wife, Jamie, who had danced in some of Jerome Robbins's companies in the 1960s. Holder would walk in cheerfully bellowing, "Ha, ha, ha, hello, Régis," in that unmistakable deep voice we all recognized from his 7UP commercial that aired constantly in the 1970s.

Those were the days when magazines grabbed you by the throat. There were no websites or email blasts or blogs. *Elle* and its competitors had to catch your eye as you strolled by a newsstand. Today's magazines, with their tiny type and blocks of information all over the page, seem confusing compared to the way *Elle* used grand gestures to garner attention. A model dressed in red from head to toe beside two words—*Red Alert!* A tightly cropped, sun-kissed face on the cover of a summer issue with the command *Face the Heat*. A portrait of an immaculately made-up brunette dressed in simple shades of beige cashmere with one word printed on the cover: *Perfect*.

Growing up with my grandparents, it seemed that elegance was perceived as *more*. My grandmother would say that her perfume, Joy, from Jean Patou, was "One hundred dollars an *ounce*. Imagine?" She'd gush about someone, "She had an engagement ring from Harry Winston the size of a golf ball." And describing a restaurant: "The steak was so enormous, Grandpa had to bring half of it home." At *Elle,* elegance meant *less*. The French said, "Americans eat too many meals" and "The tits are too big in this country."

I was one of the few Americans in the office who were accepted by the French. Most of the American staffers were treated like punching bags and couldn't do anything right. I was determined not to fall into that mold, so I listened to their opinions, watched my actions and words, and played the part. I kept up with their off-color sense of humor and was proud to be dubbed *Le Cretin Mongolien* by Régis (basically, "the stupid retard" in English). I loved getting his attention knowing that the people he was *not* interested in were completely ignored. I remember one of the saucier gals warning me to be careful of a tacky editor, saying to me in a smoky voice, "If she tells you that you look nice today, you go home and burn all of your clothes." Knowing a bit of French, I'd chuckle as I overheard comments like *"Oh là là, quelle fesse"* (What an ass) or *"Sa robe est affreux"* (Her dress is hideous).

The non-French part of the staff was made up of hardworking New Yorkers who had worked at other magazines and were responsible for getting *Elle* out the door every month despite the Europeans' "work habits." These poor souls were kept waiting until noon for the French to arrive at work or for film from a shoot to arrive at Kennedy airport, then they were challenged to write an editorial essay to accompany a close-up photo of a model's bare ass. I remember the beauty editor staring at one of these booty numbers from all angles and saying, "I guess I can talk about moisturizing after the beach . . . ?"

As I hunched over my drawing board doing mechanicals (the pre-Macintosh way a magazine was made), the stories I heard were incredible. There was a wedding in Ibiza where a top Hachette executive and his bride took their vows in the nude. A famous photographer took his giant penis from his pants and shook it in front of a group of bikini-clad models in order to get an animated reaction. An older, attractive blonde editor invited her town car driver up to her apartment after a long day at the office.

My buddies on the floor would call me the "house servant." There were hazards in being the house servant. I remember once being transfixed by the ember of Melka Tréanton's cigarette as she gestured flamboyantly while telling a long story. Melka was a legend in the fashion world; she discovered Jean Paul Gaultier and Thierry Mugler. Just as she finished her story, her hand flew back and her cigarette went sizzling into my forearm. "*Je m'excuse,*" she said offhandedly. I've never been so proud of something so painful.

I was the diplomat between the two continents. Régis would send me to the editor with something like "Matt, go to Marian and tell her that this word is too long to do a nice layout." Shooting the messenger, Marian would shout, "You go tell Régis it's a duck in a *tangerine* sauce! There is no shorter word for *tangerine*!"

Being the link between the two continents provided me with lots of time with the magazine's senior editors, and I lingered in their offices whenever I could. At first, my behavior was extremely polite and respectful. I remember a chic Italian editor, an Olivetti heiress, once saying to me, "Matt, how did you get to be so good-natured?" I walked away immediately thinking that "good-natured" was a word you'd use to describe a dog's disposition. I was beginning to be pigeonholed as the benevolent servant boy to these connoisseurs, and I was anxious to become an equal.

My family hated snobs and often spoke about *real* people or *good* people; they had no interest in high society. In 1980 I was with my parents in Heathrow airport waiting for a flight to New York. I was fascinated watching a wealthy-looking mother with long blonde hair, dressed in slacks and high heels, holding a giant Gucci handbag. She reminded me of Jerry Hall. She was chatting to another woman and allowing her beautiful young daughters to run wild around the waiting area, disturbing everyone. I was sitting patiently on a bench with my cousin Gary doing Mad Libs when one of the little girls asked us for some of our candy. We let her choose some from our bag, and as she skipped away, my dad said, "I don't like people like that." My parents said things like "*Who* does she think *she* is, dolled up like Marilyn Monroe?" or "I remember them when they didn't have two dimes to rub together." *Elle* editors were the opposite; appearances went *far*. Physical beauty or being a member of a famous family impressed them, but brains, style, and humor were equally valued, and I had no choice but to shoot for the latter.

I met Marian McEvoy the day she arrived in New York from Paris. She was brought in to replace the magazine's editor-in-chief, who was on her way out. After fifteen years in Paris, Marian was better suited than her predecessor had been to navigate the French mind-set. Marian came straight to the office from the airport wearing an enormous black Russian fur hat and matching hand warmer. I'd never seen anything like *that* before. She was beautiful, like a young Vivien Leigh with white skin, red lips, and a widow's peak. Her dark hair was pulled tightly back and tied with black grosgrain ribbons. On a random Tuesday she would be dressed immaculately, ready for a dinner party; Yves Saint Laurent suits, mile-high heels, and about five hundred necklaces of gigantic pearls, massive crosses, and several different gold chains. I loved Marian, and she became a big sister to me, showing me the ropes at all the big-time media hangouts like Da Silvano downtown on Sixth Avenue and Michael's on West Fifty-fifth Street. When I would reach the boiling point with the French, she'd calm me down with her sage advice over drinks at a dark corner table at The Carlyle.

My other grown-up pal at work was the fashion director, Jane Hsiang. Jane was a knockout, a former model from the '60s. She was born in China, came to New York in her teens, and was discovered by the fashion photographer Derujinsky. Jane had a small, chic apartment on Sutton Place, and for some reason she always made it clear to the staff that she was of Mandarin descent. After seeing black-and-white pictures from the 1930s of her beautiful mother, with her jet-black, bobbed hair, wearing elegant Western attire, I told Jane she was a "Merchant Ivory" Chinese person, which made her howl. There was a nude photo of Jane shot by Bill King, and though it hung prominently in her living room, Jane would run over and hide it dramatically with her body. She was outrageous, with a wide-open smile and a laugh that was actually more of a scream. She had an endless supply of stories from her modeling days, and I'd beg her to tell my favorites: flying to Los Angeles to meet with producer Albert Broccoli for a Bond girl role, and partying so hard on arrival that she slept through the audition, or rappelling off the roof of her West Village town house on her stunt-man husband's back and on the trip down accidentally catching a glimpse of her nerdy Jewish neighbors having kinky sex.

No one knew better than me how to get Jane going. She could walk into the art room completely pissed off about something and I'd change her mood in a minute, saying, "Jane, none of this matters, what *matters* is how many times your legs *alone* were in *Vogue* magazine!" Jane would immediately forget her emergency, scream, and in her Chinese accent remind everyone in the room, "Oh, you know, I had a *very* good body!" Then she'd catwalk back and forth around my desk, saying, "I have fantastic legs!"

One night I picked Jane up at her apartment for dinner. She was wearing black leather pants, a skintight tank top, and high heels. When we got into the elevator, she stepped back against the wall, put her fists on her hips, and stared straight at me: "Little Buddy, does Aunt Jane look like an old hooker?" I laughed, excited for an Aunt Jane evening. Jane was a snob and would say the most horrible things right to your face, but somehow what she said was so absurd that it was funny. Sitting at an outdoor café, Jane once said, "Little Buddy, people are made up of four things." She began to count on her fingers: "Looks, education, breeding, and talent." She gathered her fingers into a fist and drew it to her chest, saying, "I have all four. You only have two!" We both cracked up to the point of almost crying, yelling, "I have two!" and "You have four!" To this day I haven't had the courage to ask which two I had.

After working at *Elle* for four years, I felt it was time to move on. I didn't know what I wanted to do, but there was no position to grow into at *Elle,* and I felt I'd learned enough to be able to art direct a magazine myself. Feeling slightly disloyal, I phoned upstairs to the executive floor and requested a meeting with the publication director of all the magazines, Jean-Louis Ginibre. There was a bit of a rivalry among the men who worked under Daniel Filipacchi, and I felt that although Jean-Louis and I hit it off, no doubt he also liked the idea of poaching Régis's protégé. The other magazines that Jean-Louis oversaw were strong, but they lacked the flair of *Elle*. Coming from the nerve center of the company's crown jewel, I held a state secret—I knew how to design *Elle* magazine.

Over the following two years, Jean-Louis would become the most important mentor of my life while turning me into Hachette's top design gun. I loved Jean-Louis, and he treated me like a son. Several times over the years at a restaurant table, he would clasp his hands over mine and say, "Matt, I love you." When I'd laugh and squirm, trying to hide my discomfort with his honesty, he'd repeat himself as if to make sure I knew he meant it. "Matt, I love you."

Jean-Louis had a son named Jean-Noel, who was my age and felt like a long-lost, long-distance brother to me. Jean-Louis would fill me in on what was going on in his life, always reminding me, "Matt, he is *Jewish* like you, his mother is *Jewish*!" I would ask, "If he's Jewish, why did you name him Jean-Noel, like *Christmas*?" When Jean-Noel was in town I would play down how close Jean-Louis and I had become; I'd say, "I've already got a father, he's all yours." Jean-Louis and I attacked each new project together: the redesign of an interiors magazine, a custom project for Sony, or, in spring 1995, the top-secret logo design prototype for a new political magazine. After a few days of working on it, I had a good idea of what my next task would be.

"Matt, wear a jacket on Monday, I would like to invite you to lunch," Jean-Louis said, sounding like Maurice Chevalier. He knew if he didn't tell me to wear a jacket, I'd stroll into work in my newest uniform of Levi's corduroys and a navy crew-neck sweater. Asking me to wear a jacket meant he had something important to discuss. On Monday, I met Jean-Louis at his usual place, Le Bernardin, on West Fifty-first Street. We sat at his usual spot, table number one, and the waiter poured the wine. He stopped the waiter when there were two drops in my glass. "Do not give him too much, he has to work today." The owner of the restaurant, Maguy Le Coze, came over and kissed J.L. on both cheeks as he introduced me for the fifth time. J.L. put his arm around her waist and wagged his finger at her, saying, "Make sure you are here next Wednesday. I am coming to lunch with a major celebrity."

Having been in the magazine business for forty years, J.L. was blasé about stars. But that day he acted cagey and secretive. After a few slabs of buttery monkfish, he confirmed my hunch. "Matt, I think we are close to a deal with Kennedy." He gulped his wine. The whole town was buzzing with John F. Kennedy Jr. sightings as he went from publishing house to publishing house looking for a partner to launch his political magazine. "If you like, next week you can meet him, and if he likes you, maybe you can work with him." Feeling that this was a long shot, I guess I didn't look sufficiently excited. Jean-Louis began to tease, "Imagine, Matt, 'I am working with John Kennedy,'" trying to get a reaction. He wiped his mouth with his napkin and raised his eyebrows, saying, "My boss, John," and then, "My friend, John . . ."

I was more interested in musicians and movie stars than politicians. I hadn't followed the Kennedys over the years and didn't know anything about John. After working for years with two great design mentors, I knew I was qualified for the job but was apprehensive about working with a celebrity. Jean-Louis reminded me that John had never worked in magazines before, and he would be learning from us. Still, I was concerned about how John would behave and what he'd be like to work with every day. I went to the bookstore and bought a paperback called *Prince Charming* to try to get a sense of who I'd be working with. It was all very abstract, so I decided to wait and see what would happen.

Three weeks later, the deal was done and Jean-Louis assigned me the task of designing the logo for John's new magazine, *George*. I didn't get much direction about what I was supposed to create. All I knew was that Hachette needed a logo and a prototype fast in order to start selling advertising for a fall launch. I gathered strong images that I found mostly in British men's magazines like *The Face* and *Arena* and started to place the letters G-E-O-R-G and E in different fonts to see what felt right. I began to fill my wall with dozens of mock *George* covers with different logos. I was shooting in the dark. I didn't know much about John F. Kennedy Jr., politics, or who exactly would buy this magazine, but I knew what I liked to look at, and I went with my gut.

JFK Jr. was temporarily housed in a conference room in the Hachette building. I was in an office down the hall, with a Xerox machine outside my door. I couldn't concentrate, because the copier was constantly in use; either all the Xerox machines at Hachette had suddenly broken down or word had spread that you could catch a glimpse of John if you stood there long enough.

The phone rang one morning. It was J.L. "Matt, I would like to bring John Kennedy to look at the logos you are designing." I put on my sport coat and sat at my computer, trying to crank out even more solutions than I had already. Within a few minutes, Jean-Louis appeared at my door with John. "John, I would like you to meet Matt Berman." As I shook John's hand, I noticed that our hands were similar in size, and we exchanged a nice, firm handshake. His gaze was open, honest, and nonjudgmental. I was immediately at ease and knew I was in the presence of a kind person.

I never really read that book I'd bought about John. I skimmed over a few chapters but mainly studied the pictures in the center of the book for any signs of what he might *really* be like. The photos didn't tell me much; it was the same selection you see today when you Google *JFK Jr*—John with Jackie, John peeking out from under President Kennedy's desk, John saluting President Kennedy's casket, and the usual beefcake photos of John with his shirt off. The book shed no light on the real John and I didn't know anyone who knew him, so I did what I always do when I'm lost: I turned to astrology—even though I know it's bullshit. I went to the Strand bookstore and sat on a stool scouring through books about star signs. John was a Sagittarius and I am a Gemini. According to the books, we were astrological opposites and a perfect match. Reading further that Sagittarius is a fire sign and Gemini is an air sign, I decided to wait for the flames.

The few celebrities I'd seen around New York never looked the way I expected. I spotted Madonna once, and she was pretty but tiny. I was on a checkout line with Ed Norton, and he came across as someone you might have gone to high school with. When I saw John Kennedy for the first time, there was no disappointment. I studied the familiar face I'd seen in so many photographs. Large, wide-spaced brown eyes, arching down toward the sides of his face, like his mother's. Thick, wavy hair like his father's. The features were so familiar. There was nothing ordinary about John. He looked like a movie star.

In my office that day, John commented as I enlarged each logo to the size of my computer screen. "That one looks like a skateboarding magazine." "That one is kind of fashiony; too thin or something." "That one's *kind* of cool, try it with a little *g*." Leaning back in his chair, he confessed, "I'm kind of bad at this stuff. Which one do you guys like?"

I was distracted by an *Arena* magazine on my desk with Daryl Hannah on the cover. John had dated her; it had been in the tabloids. I was uncomfortable and didn't want him to think I'd been reading up on him. The magazine was inches from John's hand. Still looking at the screen, he reached over and turned it facedown. We agreed to take a break and look with fresh eyes later on.

Hours later, I got a call from Araminta, the receptionist. "Matt," she said in her impossibly slow Southern drawl, "John Kennedy is at reception for you." She could have gotten the name wrong; she once forwarded me a call from Richard *Avelon*'s studio (not to be confused with Richard *Avedon*, the world-famous photographer). I ran out to get him. "Hey, Matt, I wanted to ask you if you'd mind if my girlfriend takes a look at those logos later. She's a little more into that stuff than I am." I thought, *It's all over; she works at Calvin Klein and knows the coolest people in town. She's going to have me replaced with one of her fancy friends.* "No problem," I said.

Half an hour later, I was eating potato chips in my dismal gray-carpeted office, glad to have a moment to myself. I took a sip of Snapple and turned to see a beautiful woman leaning into my doorway. "Are you Matt?" she asked. I looked up, squinting in the harsh fluorescent light. Great, she had caught me smeared with potato chip grease. She came into the office and offered her hand and a huge smile. "Hi, I'm Carolyn." She was gorgeous in a flowered summer dress and high heels. Wavy dirty-blonde hair framed her face. She crouched close behind me, her face almost resting on my shoulder as we looked at the logos together. She smelled incredibly good. Thrusting her hand into my bag of chips, she said, "I'm starving, can I have some?" "Ooh, I like that one!" she said, smudging my screen with one hand and brushing crumbs off my body with the other. Later, she told John, "The logos are young, cool, they look exactly right."

I was in love. And I got the job.

2.

SQUARE DANCING FOR JEWISH SINGLES

We were an unlikely team. John was confident, charismatic, the son of the most beloved president in history. I was self-conscious, self-deprecating, and son of the most beloved restaurant supplier in all of Fairfield County, Connecticut. John loved football in the park on a Saturday; I loved a good *Twilight Zone* marathon on cable. He loved *Forrest Gump*; I thought it was corny. When I was blearily hitting the snooze button at seven in the morning, he was plunging into the Hudson River in a kayak. This split-screen idea always made us laugh. After one of John's sporty weekends, he'd say, "Matt, I was double-parked in front of your building for two hours on Friday. You said you'd be downstairs with your ice-climbing gear!" John thought I was the sort of freak who was either working at *George* or hibernating in my apartment, which during those years was not far from the truth.

We spent so many long days working closely together that my first impressions of an intimidating, larger-than-life John changed and he became someone I was completely and unconditionally comfortable with. My brothers, Brad and Andy, who are eight and five years older than me, always seemed so cool: going to rock concerts in New York or flying to Colorado to ski with their pack of grungy friends. I felt that way about John, a brother who led an impossibly cool life.

I recently found an old answering machine tape of John calling me on a Saturday, saying, "Hey, Vampire, come on, lift the coffin door." He mimicked the creaking sound of a hinge opening. "Don't be scared, Vampire, come on, get out of the coffin, walk over to the telephone." John had gotten to know me so intimately that he could really make me laugh.

Our joking brought us even closer together, and John schlepped me around like a kid brother. Once I was at John's apartment picking up something I needed for a shoot and John said, "Come to dinner with me; it's Carolyn's nana's birthday." I felt awkward crashing an intimate family dinner. We walked over to Little Italy to a small, old-time pasta place. Waiting inside were Carolyn, her best friend, Jessica Weinstein, RoseMarie from the office, and Carolyn's grandmother. Nana was a tiny, frail version of Carolyn and lived in Ossining. RoseMarie asked her if she was scared living so close to

Sing Sing prison. In a world-weary New York way she answered, "Sweetheart, trust me, if someone breaks out of jail in Ossining, the last thing they're going to do is stay in Ossining." Carolyn had spent the afternoon shopping at Barney's with Nana and told us that when she tried on a pair of high-heel Prada pumps, Nana shouted across the shoe salon, "Carolyn, take those off, you look like a prostitute!" Nana reminded me of my aunt Rose from Parkchester, making John's world feel that much closer to mine.

Although our mothers were so different, they had both tried to teach us to be *normal*. John had such casual table manners, talking with his cheeks packed with food while grabbing fries off his dining companion's plate. I think Jackie taught him to be unspoiled, masculine, and real. He could high-five a stranger on the subway, eat with his hands, and slurp from your can of soda in a way that dispelled the image of a Little Lord Fauntleroy. I remember how embarrassed John looked when I teased him about a small photo *Hello!* magazine published of him at ten years old driving a little boat in Greece with *John* written in script on its shiny red bow.

My mom did the same, encouraging me to go on the school trips I was frightened of and to play ball with the neighborhood kids. John and I both went out of our way to make other people feel comfortable and I think it was our mothers' doing.

My own insecurities date back to the Sunday before Thanksgiving in 1964, when I was five months old. My dad had gone to the office to catch up on holiday orders. My two older brothers,

Brad and Andy, were watching *Lost in Space* on television, and I was in my carriage on our patio, unattended for a few moments. When my mother went inside to put a load of clothes into the washing machine, two raccoons jumped on top of me and began to eat me alive. Our next-door neighbors had raised the orphaned raccoons as pets. By the time my mother heard my cries and ran out to courageously pull the two twenty-pound monsters off my seventeen-pound body, I was in need of emergency surgery to put together the parts of my face that had been scratched, ripped, and slashed apart. The news made the *Stamford Advocate*.

One side of my upper lip and nose were badly scarred. Early on, the scars didn't cause me stress, because I was comfortable in the sheltered world my parents had built around me. I had seven cousins, all boys around my age, and the neighborhood kids were my friends. Everyone knew my story, and no one made me feel self-conscious. My parents told me that Dr. Dubrovnik, the plastic surgeon who had done my initial reconstructive surgery, would finish the job when my face was fully developed. Like a teenager waiting to get my braces off, I waited for the doctor to make me perfect again.

In kindergarten, I had lots of friends and even won a dance contest with a girl named Joy dancing to the song "Joy to the World." By first grade, I began answering the questions that I would hear every day for the rest of my school life: "What happened to your face?" followed by "Does it hurt?" Meaner kids, like Danny Decampo, went right for "Hey, Raccoon Face!" I remember my mom calling up Danny's mother, who looked like a *floozy* according to my mom, to get Danny to stop. That plan backfired. The next day at school, Danny warned the other kids, "Don't make fun of him or he'll tell his *mommy*."

Telling my story became automatic, and after repeating it thousands of times, it became hollow, almost trivial to me. Friends and family members offered their unconsciously hurtful thoughts and ideas, like "When you start shaving, those scars will get sanded down," or "Mr. Stern has a scar from the top of his head down to the bottom of his chin, and he has a beautiful wife," or "You'll grow a mustache one day and no one will know the scars are there." Or, my all-time favorite, "Nobody notices those scars—you're crazy!" My family and I didn't want to talk about it and probably wanted it to go away. But some things don't go away, especially things on your face.

One day, I snooped through the messy closet next to my mom's desk, looking through boxes of family photographs. I discovered a manila envelope, with *Matthew, 1964* written on it in blue ballpoint script. Squeezing the envelope, I felt some slide sheets and suspected what was inside. I distracted my dad from the television. "Can I look at this, Dad?" He replied, "Only if you want to." I slid one sheet halfway out of the envelope and held it over a table lamp. For the first time, I saw what everyone else had lived through. An African-American nurse holding me, my infant face covered in blood. It was hard to tell exactly what was going on, how bad the damage was. I slid the sheet out farther and started to feel sick as the images on the slides zoomed closer in on my tiny face. I'd seen enough; my dad and I agreed we would throw them away, and so we did.

As I grew more and more self-conscious, I tried covering my face with my hands as much as possible. I always had a hand near my face—biting my nails, rubbing my hands on my face when I laughed, and *always* resting the scarred side of my face on my fist at a desk or a table. I wore long bangs, hoping to cover my scars, and even tried to disguise the flaws with cover-up sticks from the makeup department of the drugstore. I even ordered some plastic nose putty from an ad in the back of a comic book to try to patch up the missing parts. My desperate efforts sent the message to my parents that it was time to deal with the inevitable plastic surgery.

When I was eleven, arrangements were made for Dr. Dubrovnik to operate on me. I was excited because I believed the doctor could magically return my face to normal. The Sunday before the operation was scheduled at Greenwich Hospital, I came into the house and was stopped short by my mom's heartbroken face. With a catch in her voice, she told me, "Matthew, Dr. Dubrovnik died on the tennis court today." I looked to my grandmother, who stood behind my mom and confirmed the news with a nod, adding, "Well, at least he didn't drop dead halfway through operating on you!" She had a point.

A freak accident I had no recollection of had screwed up my

life. It wasn't until recently, while writing this book, that I realized John and I had that in common too—before we were old enough to remember, we both suffered an irreversible tragedy that colored the rest of our lives. Before John appeared on *Oprah,* he had asked her in advance *not* to show any childhood pictures of him. Despite his request, the famous picture of John as a toddler saluting his father's casket was projected on a screen behind them. John came back to the office after the show and told me she had shown that picture and said, "I was three years old, I have no memory of doing that."

Nor did I have any recollection of November 22, 1964, the day I was attacked by raccoons—one year to the day after President Kennedy's assassination on November 22, 1963. John and I both lived under the enormous shadow of events we had no control over and could not remember. I was always the kid who was eaten by raccoons, and he was always JFK's son. We both got attention for the wrong reasons.

Of course, John's face was perfect. Jean-Louis once brought a famous Indian plastic surgeon named Rajan to the *George* offices to meet him. I stood to the side and watched as this guy marveled at John's face to the point of making John so uncomfortable that he started scratching his nose to break the man's trance. He was flawless. Being scarred myself made me hypersensitive to physical flaws in others; I immediately notice imperfections on people I pass on the street—a scar, a missing finger, or a bad nose job. John had the ability to see inner flaws in people, and always responded with empathy. He'd make a beeline for the shyest person in the room and talk to them. He'd engage someone he could tell was nervous about meeting him by asking them a question that was easy to answer; a strategy I attribute to Jackie's parenting.

I was sensitive, even empathetic, but I was never sure who I was, so I became a chameleon. If my mom liked raspberry jam, so did I. If my grandmother thought Goldie Hawn laughed like an idiot, so did I. If the French loved *Twin Peaks,* so did I. In reality, I prefer cherry jam, I love Goldie Hawn, and I never really got *Twin Peaks*. It was much easier to mirror people than to confront our differences.

I dreaded school. If I had a few extra minutes in the morning, I'd lie on the floor with Chumley, our English bulldog, who slept by the sliding glass window in our living room, snoring. I wished I could trade places with him and not deal with the day ahead of me.

I was tired of being different, and I tried to camouflage myself by dressing in navy sweatshirts, green army pants, and white Stan Smiths. I hated getting haircuts because I felt exposed; short hair revealed my face, so I kept my hair long. When I was called on in class, my voice would crack from a combination of nerves and my not having spoken since my morning arrival. By junior high, I had become so withdrawn at school that I let a teacher call me Mark instead of Matt for a whole semester without correcting her. In gym class, I wasn't the *last* kid picked for the team, like the fat kid, or the skinny geek with glasses, but I wasn't far behind. I learned how to completely avoid situations that might be difficult or embarrassing. I spent lunchtime reading in the library, avoiding the politics and trauma of the school lunchroom. I became so good at being invisible that the kids never even wondered where I was.

I ultimately found the thing that would help me relieve the stress. I could draw well and loved doing pencil sketches of beautiful faces, erasing and redrawing the curve of a cheek or the edge of a lip until the image was just right. Being able to make things perfect was therapeutic for me. One night when I was in fourth grade, I went to see *The Three Musketeers* with my parents. I came to school the next day and drew a detailed line drawing of the film's star, Raquel Welch, in the center of my desk. As the weeks and months went by, the drawing became more and more elaborate until every corner of the desk was covered with scenes from the movie. I became a celebrity at school after my teacher, Mrs. Levine, proudly invited teachers and children in to see *my* desk. Mrs. Levine guarded the desk like a lioness and warned the cleaning crew not to touch it. The last day of school the whole class gathered to watch the custodian scrub the drawing away with Ajax, restoring the desk to its faux wood-grain Formica surface. I wish someone had taken a picture of it.

Despite my social unease, life with my family was comfortable for me, and I kept it completely separate from my school life. I never invited the few friends that I made in school to my house.

I cherished my private time with my parents and cousins. My mom had opened an antiques shop with some girlfriends, and I spent most weekends with her and my dad touring antiques shows around New England. I became pals with all the regular freaks at those shows, like the dumpy blonde vintage-clothing dealer who strolled around her booth in a gold lamé evening gown once owned by Jean Harlow or the New England hippie who specialized in circus-related antiques and displayed a terrifying four-foot-tall moving mechanical ringmaster complete with a black beaver top hat, red velvet tails, and a miniature whip. I spent those days searching the booths for movie stills, art deco clocks, top hats, and anything Bauhaus. Antiquing led to art projects, like building a model stage set of a 1930s apartment out of cardboard. I would wake each morning excited about the changes I'd make on the apartment. I'd go to the library to research Bauhaus buildings; how could I make plastic look like frosted glass? What aluminum tape could I buy at the hardware store to make stainless steel columns?

For years I walked the line between the shy, frightened raccoon kid in class and the artistic kid who could draw. I found it exhausting to maintain that dichotomy between the quiet kid and the artist, but in eighth grade the two personalities finally began to merge. I started drawing cartoons of all my teachers. The grouchy, bony science teacher, Miss Hanley, became a skeleton with earrings, bell-bottom pants, and platform sandals. Miss Bertolini, the pretty

English teacher, was rendered voluptuously in a bikini like a pinup girl. Mr. Fontana, with his thick mustache, was transformed into a Hells Angels biker. The kids would gather around me and laugh as I added telltale details to each drawing. The sketches eventually made their way out of the art room, and the teachers ambushed me in the hall, with a shaking fist from Miss Hanley, nuggies from Mr. Fontana, and the hairy eyeball from Miss Bertolini. Turned out the kid who drew a lot and never talked in class was *funny*! I'd broken a spell, and I liked the feeling.

Seeing the effect art had on me, my mom sought out after-school classes in everything from filmmaking to ceramics. She enrolled me in all of them, leaving no afternoon empty. Marthe Clamage, a local sculptor who taught art at the local high school and gave art classes in her garage, was my favorite. The place was jammed with worktables, garbage cans full of clay, two kilns, reams of different drawing papers, paints, charcoals, and artifacts from her travels—hats, masks, statues, and woven tapestries. I was always amazed, because my aunt and uncle lived on the same street in an identical split-level house, but Marthe's house felt like another world.

Marthe was in her fifties, with pale skin, strong features, curly black hair, and glasses. She was married to a kind businessman named Allan, and although she had three kids of her own, she always gave her undivided attention to the kids she taught. She'd confront the black kids from the projects who were constantly blowing off her class, or showing up and not performing. "Africa is such an incredibly rich artistic culture!" she'd exclaim, putting a ball of clay in their hands. "I know you have it in you!"

The provincial wives in town thought she was a kook. "She doesn't wear a stitch of makeup," they'd say, and "Her clothes are from the year one." She was a bohemian trapped in the suburbs. Marthe became my first adult friend. We'd go on adventures together in her broken-down Lincoln Continental, visiting artists' studios, or a tag sale, or exploring a colonial cemetery I'd found.

One Friday afternoon when Marthe was driving me home, I asked her, "What are you and Mr. Clamage doing tonight?" She replied, "I have my play group. A few friends are coming over, and we're each going to read different parts." "That's *so* corny!" I said, slapping my forehead in disbelief. "Well, maybe people think going to tag sales and cemeteries is corny," she said, pulling into my driveway. Marthe didn't give a shit what anyone thought, including me, and I loved that.

She was the first person to teach me to have confidence in my talent and enjoy the things that interested me instead of worrying about being judged for them. I remember asking her what I should be when I grew up. An architect, a painter, a stage set designer, a movie director? She just waved her hand dismissively. "Pick anything. Someone like you will thrive in anything you choose."

Marthe had had breast cancer when I first met her and had gotten a mastectomy. Of course, she took it in stride, as she did everything else in her life. When my mother and her girlfriends visited her after her operation, Marthe did a vaudeville-style shimmy and asked, "Okay, girls, which one's the falsie?"

My senior year of high school, her breast cancer came back violently. The last time I saw her, I had phoned and asked if she needed anything. She said no, but I insisted she had to need *something*. Appeasing me, she said, "Bring me some pears," and then coughed out, "The front door is unlocked." I walked into her house and heard her weak voice call, "I'm in the bedroom." I stood far from the bed in the dark. "Where are my pears?" she asked. "Oh my God, I forgot them." I felt like an asshole and told her I'd run out and get them. Marthe shook her head and smiled, as if to say my visit wasn't about the pears.

We talked about cancer and Marthe said, "Cancer only attacks sweet people like me." I chuckled nervously. "I'm serious," she said. "Mean people have lots of acid in their bodies that eats up the cancer." I think she was right. After she died, I was in my guidance counselor's office and found a recommendation letter Marthe had written for one of my college applications. I opened it just far enough to read the last line: "Matthew had a tragic childhood accident and has found his way in life through art." In that one sentence, Marthe reminded me that I was already whole, flaws and all.

On Tuesdays, my mom would drop me off for painting lessons taught by my great-uncle Harold, who was married to my great-aunt Ethel, my grandpa Sam's voluptuous older sister. They lived near the beach in Stamford in an old Dutch Colonial house. Uncle

Harold worked as an illustrator at Radio City Music Hall when Vincente Minnelli was the art director, and later worked for RKO and Paramount as a movie poster artist. He designed the poster for *The Barefoot Contessa,* a silky charcoal drawing of a barefoot Ava Gardner wearing an extremely low-cut evening gown and being embraced by a lover from behind. His other masterpiece was for the 1933 film *Flying Down to Rio,* which pictured a chorus line of dancing girls standing on the wing of an airplane, painted in vibrant, jewel-toned watercolor. It amazed me that in those days he could get away with not putting the faces of the film's stars, Fred Astaire and Dolores del Rio, on the poster.

Uncle Harold was a Russian immigrant who lived the life of a bohemian artist while Aunt Ethel brought home the bacon with a full-time secretarial job at the courthouse. He was slim, around seventy years old at the time, with blue eyes and light yellow-blond hair that he dyed himself in the bathroom. He was a bit of an egomaniac and told tall tales of his Hollywood days, even though he hadn't left Stamford in years. Admiring a poster he'd done for *It Happened One Night,* I asked, "Uncle Harold, did you meet Clark Gable when you painted this?" Uncle Harold looked at me in disbelief and said, in his thick Russian accent, "Of course I did." I pressed him, asking "Where?" Frustrated, he answered, "At my office in New York!" When I tried to verify the story with Grandma Marcia, who couldn't stand her brother-in-law, she waved her hand dismissively. "He's full of shit. He never met anybody."

Grandma had no patience for Harold's bragging and couldn't stand that I found Aunt Ethel and Uncle Harold interesting. When I told Grandma about a fun afternoon I had at Uncle Harold's, she silently filed her nails, rolled her eyes, and chimed in with "And was Ethel home too? Did she tell you how gorgeous and sexy she was when she was young?" From the painting in the stairwell of Aunt Ethel in her 1920s flapper days, it seemed possible to me. "Was she, Grandma?" Throwing down her nail file, she sputtered, "Look, who the hell knows? She was *artistic* looking!"

Uncle Harold was a sex maniac; his conversation was peppered with big breasts, long legs, and sexual innuendo. He complained that Aunt Ethel didn't like sex as much as he did, and she'd belt back, "The night we were married, he locked me in our room and we had nothing *but* sex for days!"

Their door was usually open when I walked up to their house. I'd hear the sound of the television playing from his bedroom, that annoying song and the nerve-wracking bells they rang when someone was asked to "Come on down" on *The Price Is Right*. I'd climb the stairs and enter his room; he and Aunt Ethel had their own bedrooms. I'd nudge Uncle Harold awake. He'd get up with a bolt of energy and we'd head to his studio, which was on the other side of the hallway. I don't know how he decided what we would paint on any given Tuesday, but it was usually something wacky from his theatrical past; standing by his side at a twin easel, I'd shadow his every move as we drew dramatic South Seas seascapes in watercolors, ominous streets in dramatic perspective, with long shadows and lurking figures, and dozens of versions of dancing girls from Uncle Harold's golden age.

Although Mrs. Clamage dismissed Uncle Harold as a tacky technician, I learned things from him that she didn't teach and they don't teach in school, like how to draw a harem girl wearing a sarong and a bikini top with a perfectly rendered set of Hollywood knockers.

The only day I didn't have an art class scheduled was on Wednesday, when Stamford elementary schools closed at 1:15. Around 1:00 p.m., I'd start looking out the classroom window hoping to see my grandma Marcia's giant gold Cadillac DeVille make the wide turn into the school driveway and float up to the curb. She had her hair done the same day, and I could see her through the car window patting the back of her head, checking herself out in the rearview mirror. She was gorgeous and regal, a tall Russian beauty with long, pin-straight white hair, worn in a high bun like a crown.

The school bell would ring and I'd pick my younger cousin Gary up from his classroom. We'd walk past the school buses and slide onto the broad, smooth, caramel-colored seats of the DeVille. The car smelled like a combination of perfume, leather, and cigars. It was enormous, and Grandma looked miles away in the front seat. "Where do you wanna go for lunch?" she'd bellow, shifting the boat into gear. She had an old-time New York way of talking that sounded like Lauren Bacall. There were always three choices—Bird Cage at Lord & Taylor, Ondine at Bloomingdale's, or an old-fashioned restaurant called The Buttery, which was decorated with colonial-style decor. We would usually pick The Buttery to avoid Grandma's detouring to scour a white sale on our way out of one of the department stores. After lunch we'd go back to her house and watch TV, stretched out on the floor. At Grandma Marcia's, we could stay up late and watch Johnny Carson, eat Fritos, and drink Hawaiian Punch at all hours; we were allowed to pretend to smoke the cigarettes that Grandma kept in china boxes all around the house, as long as we didn't put the tobacco end in our mouths by mistake.

Grandma's home was a one-floor modern ranch house that was more like something you'd see in Palm Springs than Connecticut. Sitting with her legs crossed in her Danish armchair, Grandma would go off on one of her rants. "Look, these poor schmucks would cut off an arm, cut off a finger, anything *not* to go into the service." Admiring her ankle as she stretched one leg out and twirled her foot: "And lemme tell you something, if they needed someone to get killed first, those pitiful Jews were the ones they sent to the front lines!" Disinterested in the Russo-Japanese war, Gary and I would try to tune her out so we could hear what Fred and Barney were saying on *The Flintstones*.

She would talk to us as if we were adults, never candy-coating anything. Once, while driving Gary and me to the West Palm Beach airport after a school break visit, she reminded us, "You remember the story about the plane that crashed after takeoff into the Everglades? The survivors, the people who *survived* the crash were eaten by alligators."

Her frustrations would surface during family dinners, when she'd cry into her second Canadian Club sour about how the principal at Stamford High School came to her parents' house and begged them to let her accept a scholarship to Barnard College. Her parents refused, saying that she was their only daughter and they needed her to work in the family store. She was tough, brutally honest, and hard to please, teaching me early on how to win the attention of strong women.

Marcia's husband, Sam Shavelson, grew up on the Grand Concourse in the Bronx. Sam was a pampered mamma's boy who was cherished by his sisters, Ethel and Rose, and his doting mother, Sadie. Ethel always told us he looked like a Jewish Cary Grant, whose charm was irresistible to anyone around him. When Sam was in the premedical program at Fordham University, he worked part-time in the cigar shop in the Flatiron Building on Madison Square Park. One summer, a buddy of his invited him to the beach in Stamford to meet a group of nice Jewish girls who lived there. That day, he met my grandmother, who would eventually provide him with a job in the family business, a lifetime supply of golf clubs, cigars, expensive Scotch, and monthlong trips to Miami Beach every winter.

My mom, Debby, was born in 1934, and my aunt Bobbie in 1937. Sam spoiled his daughters with cars for their sixteenth birthdays, gold bracelet-watches for their eighteenth, and trips to Europe on the *Queen Elizabeth II* before college. I found a 16mm movie projector at a tag sale and played some home movies for my mom and grandparents that they hadn't seen in years. There was one of my mother's high school graduation party filmed in saturated Kodachrome. Leaning forward to tap the ash off her Benson & Hedges, Grandma scanned the flickering images for lost treasures. "Oh, Sam, look at that gorgeous vase, I *wish* I still had that vase. Look at those lamps, I *wish* I still had those lamps." My mom sat with her arms folded until she saw a scene of herself bouncing happily into the living room wearing a tight pink angora sweater. Cutting my grandmother off, Mom shouted, "I *wish* I still had those boobs!"

Grandma often bragged, "Your mother was the belle of the ball." When I found my mom's high school yearbook buried in a linen closet, Grandma's claim was confirmed. Each page was autographed in all directions in different colored ink with declarations of love from boys, teary good-byes from girlfriends, and encouraging notes from all of her teachers. In 1950, the Belle of the Ball left for the University of Michigan, the trunk of her burgundy Pontiac convertible filled with a rainbow of cashmere sweater sets.

Photos of my dad's side of the family look more like portraits of earnest Depression-era folks. My dad's father, August Berman, was a hardworking chemist who graduated from Yale in 1920 and married my grandmother, Adele, a stern elementary school teacher. Gus and Adele lived in an older part of town in a tall

Tudor house with dark furnishings. Adele ran the house like her classroom; when the grandchildren visited, no silliness was allowed. Gus and Adele were religious people, and although they went to synagogue regularly, they came across as Waspy in demeanor. They lacked the parts of being Jewish that were familiar to me, like nonstop talking, humor, and drama.

During my high school years, my amazing mom found the best plastic surgeon in the world, Daniel Baker, to patch me up during school breaks. Dr. Baker had been on the cover of *The New York Times Magazine* as part of a team of surgeons who used microsurgery to reconnect the severed hand of a Juilliard student. I almost fell off my bar stool at Odeon twenty years later when Carolyn Bessette brought up Dan Baker's name, saying he was the best in town. He was married to a socialite, was always in the gossip columns, and was rumored to have worked on Sharon Stone, Courtney Love, and Princess Diana.

Each winter my mom and I would drive into New York City to meet with Dr. Baker and discuss what could be done to my face during the upcoming summer vacation. I would sit in his silent waiting room trying not to make eye contact with the other people. When I did look around, the people looked relatively good, so I wondered what horrible disfigurements were lurking under their clothing. They were probably there for nose jobs or face-lifts.

Baker was kind, and his sophisticated Park Avenue office was reassuring. His confident tone made gruesome procedures like dermabrasion and skin grafting sound matter-of-fact. I appreciated the technical way he spoke to me, and I began to understand that plastic surgery wasn't magic.

Yet it felt good to be *doing* something about my scars. When we left Baker's office, Mom took me to exhibitions at the Whitney or to interesting shops we'd read about in *New York* magazine. I saw New York as a paradise full of amazing people where good things could happen. The last time I met with Dr. Baker for a consultation, he put his hand on my shoulder and said, "Matt, don't you want to go to the beach or some parties?" He was right. Enough surgery. It was time to live.

I applied to art schools, was accepted to all of them, and ended up going to Carnegie Mellon, because the best artist in my high school, John Currin, went there. He later went on to have exhibitions of his work at the Whitney and the Museum of Modern Art in Manhattan. My dad packed the car, my mom burst into tears in the driveway, and I was off on my own for the first time in my life.

Carnegie Mellon had sent a brochure with pictures of all the kids who were accepted to the class of 1982. I obsessively studied the glossy faces, and they scared me. I saw my future roommate and tried to decipher what he was like from his smile and his shirt choice. One picture really scared me. It was of a beautiful blonde tomboy with spiked rocker hair, long bangs covering one eye, a ripped T-shirt, and a bandana around her neck. The photo read, "Lina Weidlinger, New York." I made a mental note to avoid her.

Lina intimidated everyone at school, but she ended up being my best friend. Lina had grown up in a chic apartment near the UN and had gone to the international high school there. Her mom was a pretty blonde from Denmark who split her time between the city and their austere modern house in Bridgehampton. Lina's dad was a famous engineer from Europe who'd worked with Le Corbusier before coming to New York.

My next-door neighbor in the dorm was a cool engineering student and sculptor from New York named Eric Colby, who listened to Kraftwerk and rap music. These kids were so different from my cousins and the kids I knew in Stamford. Eric was raised by a *Ms.* magazine—era single mom who offered us words of wisdom in her Brooklyn accent: "Look, it would be wonderful if you can just date a *body,* but unfortunately, you have to take the whole damn person with it!" I wasn't in Stamford anymore, and I knew I would never go back.

Another good friend was a stylish girl from Chicago named Kim Aronson. Kim had a vast knowledge of art and photography and a neurotic Jewish family like mine. We would commiserate about how hard childhood was being ball-busted and henpecked by our families. Kim had a rich grandmother we called "The Flying Saucer," because she was always hovering and in Kim's business. The Flying Saucer would buy Kim four-hundred-dollar Jean Paul Gaultier dresses from a cool boutique downtown and sixty-dollar vials of Estée Lauder Night Repair at Kaufmann's department store, even though Kim was only nineteen years old. When I reconnected with Kim twenty years later, I told her that the Night Repair had been worth the money.

Lina had a problem with my preppy clothes and boring haircut and, as we became better friends, slowly did a Professor Higgins number on me. We'd talk for hours, lying on the lawn between classes. "*Matt Berman* is such a boring name," Lina said. "I thought of a better one for you." Resting on my elbows, I looked over at her with a raised eyebrow. "Oh, yeah? What is it?" I asked. "How about *Matthew Mann*?" she said. "That's retarded," I replied, and changed the subject. *Matt Berman* had lived through too much shit not to stick around for the payoff.

In 1986 I transferred from Carnegie Mellon to Parson's School of Design in New York City. Transformed from a shy suburban artist into a 1980s mod, I wore a steel-gray Perry Ellis suit over a black T-shirt and thick-framed Robert La Roche eyeglasses, which I'd obsessed over after seeing them in an ad in *Interview* magazine. I listened to Bryan Ferry, Tom Tom Club, The English Beat, and Fine Young Cannibals. I bought hundreds of magazines and was fascinated by anything European, especially anything French.

My hairstyle always got me a lot of attention, and I kept it up-to-date with a special card from art school that entitled me to a discount at Bruno Dessange, a chic hairdresser. The cool French coiffeurs and fancy clients intimidated me, but after trying to blend into the wallpaper for so many years, I liked the challenge. I always got the same style, an asymmetrical cut with the shorter side behind one ear and the longer side flopped down. It was very Flock of Seagulls. Once Jessica Lange was at the salon, and we left at the same time. I had just seen *Frances* and thought she was great. I walked behind her, awed by how beautiful she was, slowly strolling down Madison Avenue in the sunlight and stopping to look in shop windows.

There were celebrities everywhere in Manhattan. It wasn't unusual to see Laurie Anderson, John Lurie, or Lou Reed at the grocery store or pharmacy. My brother Brad, who was in law school, told me his teacher invited Debbie Harry and Blondie to class to discuss entertainment law. One night around 2:00 a.m., I spotted Andy Warhol buying ice cream at the deli on Seventh Avenue and Charles Street. Another night, toward the end of the '80s, I was eating dinner at Sugar Reef in the East Village and the waitress delayed putting in our order to tell us about the band she and her husband, the bartender, were in. I remember that when she said we should come see them, I rolled my eyes and did the "wrap it up" gesture with my finger—then felt like an asshole a year later when she was on the cover of Italian *Vogue.* The bartender and waitress were Lady Miss Kier and DJ Dmitry of Deee-Lite, who had just had a hit with "Groove Is in the Heart."

I lived at my brother Brad's apartment near Wall Street, but I hung out with my new art school friends. My closest friend was a native New Yorker named Adam, who was obsessed with rock-abilly and wore his hair exactly like Slim Jim Phantom from the Stray Cats. He wore creeper shoes, a leather jacket with an up-turned collar, and a different bandana around his neck every day. Underneath, he was a nice, nerdy Jewish kid who dragged me to clubs to see people like Robert Gordon.

My old buddy Kim from Carnegie Mellon moved to New York, and we frequented Greenwich Village hangouts like King Tut's Wah Wah Hut and The Pyramid. We liked jazz clubs like the Village Vanguard or Blue Note and trendy restaurants like Bar Lui on Broadway and Indochine on Lafayette.

This was the downtown New York of Martin Scorsese's *After Hours* and Jonathan Demme's *Something Wild,* and it was *fun.* You never knew where an evening could lead. You could meet someone for a bite at Moondance Diner in SoHo, follow them over to the Mudd Club, and end up uptown at an *American Psycho*–style place like Au Bar all in one evening.

In the spring of 1987, after graduating from Parsons, I was working in the windowless basement art department of the 92nd Street Y, a beloved cultural institution in New York. I designed posters or brochures for everything from Mostly Mozart concerts to Square Dancing for Jewish Singles. I thought the job was em-barrassing, but my boss, Stacy Apikos, was a favorite teacher of mine from Parsons. She made it fun and approved any new-wave design I came up with. Stacy was always going up against the Y's director, pushing to raise the design standards of the work we were doing.

The daily grind there was depressing. In the windowless cell, I spent the days with an awkward art director who took the job way too seriously and a kooky failed actress, Carole, who did the type-setting. Carole was nuts and would chatter the day away trying to get a rise out of anybody, saying things like "I want *more* sexual harassment on the job!" We blasted The Pretenders over and over. I felt like I was on a one-way train to Loserville, and I needed to get off at the next stop.

One day, the director had had enough of Stacy's headstrong attitude and fired her. I saw my opportunity to ditch this corny job and move on, so I quit the same day. The director, a big, overbearing dame named Susan, called me into her office and told me I was a "stupid kid" to quit. I explained to Susan that I had come there to learn from Stacy, and the job was pointless without her. Susan barked, "You won't find another job like this, buddy." I walked out onto Lexington Avenue to meet Stacy, thinking, *Is that a promise?*

As we barreled down Lexington Avenue in a cab, Stacy thanked me for sticking up for her, and we laughed about Big Susan's "You'll never work in this town again" threat. After a long, traumatized childhood and four transformative years at art school, I wanted a more exciting life, and an eighteen-thousand-dollar-a-year job in a cellar wasn't it.

3.

FULL-TILT BOOGIE

I found the glamour and excitement I'd been looking for when I landed the job at *Elle,* then I *really* upped the ante when I took the position as JFK Jr.'s creative director at *George.* I worked on the logo for the magazine for weeks, adjusting and readjusting every detail to make it perfect. Once John was good with it, I went upstairs to show it to Jean-Louis. He signaled me to stand outside his door. "Matt," he said with his hand over the receiver, "I am on the phone with Paris. Please wait a moment." I made small talk with Jean-Louis's longtime, two-packs-a-day secretary, Jacqueline. The woman had the thickest French accent in the world but had lived in Queens since arriving stateside with her GI fiancé after World War II. While we waited, Jacqueline told me how she and Jean-Louis had the same birthday. Today they had a very bad horoscope, and they were both in bad moods. I could hear Jean-Louis's raised voice through the door arguing with the chairman of Hachette, Daniel Filipacchi.

Jean-Louis was sitting behind his massive desk. He was wearing a beautiful, blue-striped Charvet shirt and polka-dot tie, and you could see the midtown skyline behind him. He spoke in French about *George* and John. Each time it was his turn to speak, he sounded more and more agitated, sputtering as he tried, and failed, to get his point across. Finally, Jean-Louis slammed his fist down on the desk, sending his pen flying out of his hand and onto the carpet. *"No!"* he shouted, emphasizing every syllable. *"Il . . . n'est . . . pas . . . comme . . . Albert . . . de . . . Monaco!"*

Filipacchi, a tycoon with a string of magazine successes, was asking Jean-Louis if publishing a magazine with Jackie and John F. Kennedy's son was like doing one with the son of Grace Kelly and Prince Rainier. Jean-Louis was offended. He knew that the son of the most-beloved American president was a far bigger draw. Jean-Louis slammed down the receiver. "They are impossible. They do not understand that JFK Jr. is *more* than a celebrity here."

Emerging from the elevator after Jean-Louis had approved the magazine's logo, I ran into John, who was walking out of the men's room with a newspaper under his arm, as usual. I smiled and told him about Jean-Louis's conversation. "He was on the phone with Daniel Filipacchi, and he was saying that you are not like Prince Albert of Monaco." John stopped in his tracks and burst out laughing. "Go back upstairs and tell *Grand-père* that *I* have hair!"

While I was holed up in my office, John was ensconced in a conference room with his business partner, Michael Berman, and his girl Friday, RoseMarie Terenzio. Rose was a smart, tough girl from the Bronx who took no grief from anyone. She was sharp, and she had the ability to walk into a room, listen for a few minutes, examine moods and body language, and deliver a perfect assessment of any situation. John relied on her judgment, saying, "She's usually right, Matt." By the time I met Rose, she and Carolyn had become like sisters. Carolyn had done a big-sister makeover on Rose, with straight Prada skirts, Miu Miu silk blouses, three-hundred-dollar haircuts at Brad Johns, and five-inch Manolo Blahnik heels.

The rest of the editorial staff was mostly made up of Waspy Ivy Leaguers, good students from upper-middle-class backgrounds who were extremely political and watched every move that took place in the office. For someone working at a political magazine, I knew next to nothing about politics—my friends thought it was hilarious. A few of the editors, on the other hand, often dismissed me as John's *airheaded creative director* and pegged Rose as his *dumb secretary.* Some made fun of us, but because Rose was privy to everything going on with John and I was privy to anything to do with Hachette and Jean-Louis, they knew we had power, and they showered us with invitations to lunch, drinks, and dinner. We enjoyed the attention, but we knew in our hearts that we could only trust each other.

Rose and I ate out together three nights a week to decompress after work. Eating in restaurants so often, we made up some rules we obey to this day: Never order french fries or anything chocolate; someone else will order them and offer you some of theirs. Always order a regular Coke, because only fat people drink Diet Coke and we don't want to act like fat people. Over the years, we developed our own secret language. *Gretchen Mol is coming down* meant the annoying, suburban financial lady was coming down to see us. Actress Gretchen Mol had been on a *Vanity Fair* cover wearing a sheer gown that revealed her nipples; the financial lady had once sexed herself up for a meeting with John, wearing a revealing sweater that had reminded us of that cover. *Full-tilt Boogie* meant someone was really busy. That came from the time I called to see whether Marian McEvoy could talk and her secretary, Gina, warned me in a Staten Island accent, "Sweetie, give it half an hour, it's Full-tilt Boogie down here." *We'll lose this house* meant that somebody had done something stupid with potentially bad consequences. That came from the time Rose got a speeding ticket and her Bronx dad, overreacting, had said, *"We'll lose this house!"* To this day, she and I can have an entire conversation that no one else could possibly understand.

Rose was once on a roll and nearing the climax of one of her stories when I heard a faint cry from John's office. "Rosie? Where's

Rosie?" She stopped her chattering and threw her arms up in the air, letting them land with a slap on her thighs as she announced, "The *baby's up,* better go feed him!" I burst into laughter, walked out of my office, and ran right into John. Left out of the joke, he begged us to tell him what we were laughing at. When Rose told him, John looked at both of us, angry that we were enjoying a joke at his expense. "I'm a baby?" His voice got louder. "*I'm* a baby? Matt Berman is the biggest baby that ever lived! If I make *one* comment, just *one* comment about any of his work, he whines and cries!" He was right. One time, he indulged the Hachette executives when they said the covers would sell better if we didn't disguise the stars with elaborate costumes. I didn't speak to him for a week. When we shot a lame cover of Robert Duvall on a brown background, I pouted about it for days.

Behind Rose's desk there was a low 1970s-style lounge chair, where John would relax as he dictated a letter to Rose or edited some text. When you walked up to Rose's desk, a short wall in front of her made it hard to see the chair, and I always forgot it was there. Thinking the coast was clear, I'd walk up to Rose and start spewing, "That fucking asshole so-and-so said this," or "I can't friggin' believe John doesn't like this or that." Despite Rose's desperate facial contortions attempting to warn me of his presence, I'd hear a voice from behind her. "No, no, continue, Maestro, I want to hear, who's an asshole?" I never learned my lesson, and it happened dozens of times.

Once Rose and I had a huge argument over something I can't even remember. I decided to stop talking to her, and for a time, we passed each other silently in the hall without making eye contact. We avoided being in the same room together. Rose found herself crying about the fight at John and Carolyn's place one night. With Carolyn pulling Kleenex from a box, Rose gagged out the story, and John offered her his *soothing* thoughts. "You should really be flattered that Matt isn't talking to you. Matt doesn't even take the time to be mad at anyone. He must really care about you." John hit the nail on the head, but I don't think it helped Rose at the time. She later told me that she and Carolyn looked at each other in disbelief that John had found a way to defend me. Taking the silent treatment into a second week, I started to feel that maybe I was going too far. As I entered my office, I looked over at Rose, who was seated outside John's door, and gave her a pitiful little wave and a clenched smile. Rose cocked her head to one side and thrust her middle finger at me in the most violent bird-flip I'd ever seen. Then she grabbed her cigarettes and strode into my office for a laugh-filled reconciliation.

We both loved working at *George.* I came to Hachette each morning inspired to do something great that was unlike the rest of the titles on the newsstand. I sat at my computer and stared at the logo I had designed, wondering what the rest of the magazine should look like. The only input John gave me was a black portfolio binder, a sort of scrapbook in which he compiled images he liked from newspapers and magazines. I found most of the clippings dull and feared that if this was the kind of stuff he was planning to use in the magazine, I'd have to find a way to make it look cool.

John and the Hachette executives kept saying it was a *nonpartisan political magazine,* but no one could really say what that meant or how it should look. I was on my own. I reviewed a pile of layouts that several graphic designers, including some famous ones, had sent John in hopes of getting the creative director job. George Lois, the genius behind *Esquire*'s classic 1970s covers, including the iconic image of Andy Warhol drowning in a Campbell's soup can, had turned in a six-column layout that had sort of looked like *Time* magazine. Boring. Another guy from *Interview* had submitted a layout that looked remarkably like *Interview.* It was up to me to figure out something new.

John wanted to use the tagline "Not just politics as usual" on the cover to catch the attention of people who might not be interested in politics and to make the link between politics and popular culture. I knew what *Time* looked like, and I knew what *Vanity Fair* looked like, but *George* needed an entirely different aesthetic.

I remembered what Marian McEvoy had taught me at *Elle*: "Just say yes, and then do what you want. What people aren't familiar with, they criticize." *George* was original and veered from the accepted notion of what a political magazine should be. The Hachette executives, Jean-Louis, and John had a lot at stake. They trusted me to produce something that worked; I had to trust my instincts. With that in mind, I started designing a prototype that the advertising department could use to sell the first issue of *George*.

After years of working with great editors and graphic designers who had taught me well, I was determined to find a new formula that would hold readers' attention on each and every page. The most difficult subjects to make visually attractive had to be fat Capitol Hill politicians in dark suits. But why couldn't we photograph politicians like they were movie stars? Did the images have to be old guys sitting behind desks or walking up marble steps? We were doing something new, and I wanted to figure it out organically, not fall into the accepted norms of what a magazine was.

I loved the work of the British photographer Nick Knight, who still has a cult following, and I made fake layouts using his photographs. He'd done a graphic shot of two guys head to head, screaming at each other. John figured out an article to go with the image. Using Nick's photos as the springboard, we fell into a system that worked. I would come up with visuals that had impact, and John would think up the editorial to accompany the images. "How about this great photo of a saxophone, John?" John responded, "How about *Everything You Wanted to Know about Sax: Bill Clinton Rates His Top Ten Favorite Sax Men?*" John was a natural with wit and words. He didn't overthink things. We both went with our guts and focused on making the prototype a tool that would give advertisers a sense of what the magazine would feel like.

Unable to decide on a cover concept for the prototype, we used a pale blue logo on a darker blue page, but no image. That way, we wouldn't get locked into an idea we weren't one hundred percent behind. John and I mocked up a dozen different layouts. I scanned in some Armani and Ralph Lauren advertising to place in the mock-up, and we had it printed for the *George* sales staff to go out and pitch. The response was much stronger than any of us expected, which sent us scrambling to come up with more editorial pages to balance all of the incoming ads.

With the prototype out there and the advertising rolling in, John began assembling his staff. John or Hachette must have felt that *George* needed a seasoned editor, so they hired a guy named Eric Etheridge who had held senior positions at *Rolling Stone* and the *New York Observer*. The essays and interviews were John's and Eric's domain. I handled the visual ideas, and I did my best to include Eric in whatever I was doing. If I came into the office with sketches of editorial ideas for John, I left a duplicate stack on Eric's desk. *How about photos of the contents of politicians' wallets? Architects' ideas to redesign the White House? Recipes of the first ladies?*

John loved seeing the progress and saved piles of the ideas he liked. It didn't take long before I realized that Eric thought of me as a young, green art director of little consequence—an intuition that was proven to me when I saw his duplicate stack of my ideas in his trashcan. Once, stepping on my toes, he invited the well-known director of photography from another magazine to meet John. John knew this was uncool and made sure I was at the meeting too. It was the first time of many that John would step in to protect me.

One time, when Eric was leading another dull editorial meeting, John and I ended up sitting on the floor with our backs against a desk. As in every magazine office, desktops were a jumble of photos, layouts, and free samples from various companies, offering up everything from cosmetics to sneakers. While Eric droned on about pundits, swing votes, and wonks, John reached his hand backward over our heads and pulled down some Kiehl's hair cream. He squeezed a blob into his hand and did his best Fonzie imitation, smoothing the cream on each side of his head with a James Dean squint. Eric was oblivious. After a few issues Eric was gone.

While I was getting to know something about office politics, real politics still didn't interest me. During those first months at *George,* I was in between apartments and staying in the spare room of my friend Peggy Russell, who worked at *Elle Decor* (and is now the editor-in-chief of *Architectural Digest*). Peggy and I had started at Hachette at the same time and had become like brother and sister. Knowing I was now at a political magazine, she made sure I was ready for work each day by briefing me on the latest news stories. Toweling off in the bathroom, I'd hear Peggy shout from the kitchen table as she turned pages of the *New York Times,* "Madeleine Albright was named first female secretary of state, Matt." Hearing no reaction, she said, "Matt, *please* don't say, 'Who's Madeleine Albright?'" Other times, she'd throw me a bone, knowing I was more comfortable discussing pop culture: "Matt, Hugh Grant was arrested with a prostitute in his car."

When I was given the lineup of editorial stories for the first issue of *George*, I recognized few of the names on the list. I went to John's office for help, and he made it easy. "This is an article about the Native American senator Ben Nighthorse Campbell, who rides Harleys." I drew a picture of a man flying down the highway with wind in his hair. "Who's Candace Gingrich, John?" He chuckled. "She's Newt's half sister, an outspoken lesbian." I drew a portrait of a stern-looking female, then pinned the drawings to my office wall. Within a few days, my wall was papered with a complete issue of *George* in black Sharpie.

The next step was to turn the drawings into photographs. Booking photographers wasn't easy, because the magazines at Condé Nast, *Vogue* and *Vanity Fair*, had many of the best locked up with exclusive contracts. If they weren't on contract there, they were signed with *Rolling Stone*. I flipped through my prototype with Nick Knight's images and some from other new British talent and thought, *Why not just hire these guys?* Piles of portfolios arrived at the office from established photographers, but most of them looked academic—weary photographs of old faces, some dried-up hands and a watch, some old books on a desk, a geezer wearing a garden hat in the yard at his country house.

I decided we'd hire only the highest level of photojournalists, guys from the legendary Magnum Photos agency like Bruce Davidson, Alex Webb, and James Nachtwey. For the rest of the portraits we'd use completely unknown photographers. There were two guys in particular who photographed things in an original way: British kids named Jake Chessum and Platon Antoniou (who goes by Platon). I'd seen a few of their photos in the British magazine *i-D* and flew them to New York. *George* would give them their first shots at mainstream exposure. These guys were so thrilled to have the opportunity that any setup worked for them, even a friend's sofa. They would become good friends of mine, flying back and forth across the Atlantic as we attacked *George*'s tough subjects, from Capitol Hill fogies and frumpy socialites to milquetoast incumbents. They always returned from their trips with a fresh point of view. The way they saw these political stars was so funny to me. In their British accents they'd recount, "Well, he wasn't exactly a matinee idol," or "Yeah, she was all right, nice old lady," and "That one had a face like a bag a hammers."

Working on a magazine start-up was exciting, fast-paced, and sometimes glamorous, but it was also a race against time. There was a deadline for the prototype, a deadline for the advertising to be sold and placed for the first issue, and a deadline for the magazine to be on the newsstand. The *George* office was a circus from 10:00 a.m. to 7:00 p.m. There were always interruptions, visitors coming through to meet John or look at what we were doing, someone who had to "run something past John" or just had to "nab him for a minute." The lady in charge of circulation once came in and cornered John, saying that she lived in a racially diverse neighborhood in Brooklyn and that naming the magazine after a slaveholder like George Washington offended her. I came to his aid and said, "Come on, John, what does *she* care? Madeleine is Jewish! In 1790 she was pushing a junk cart around a *shtetl* in Poland!"

John's family and celebrity friends provided frequent distraction. On a random day at *George*, John's sister, Caroline, might drop something off, his brother-in-law, Edwin Schlossberg, might run up to have a look around the office, Sheryl Crow might pop in to see her portrait. John had hired Norman Mailer to write an article, and I did a double take when I saw him crammed into a cubicle, telling an intern, "Oh, nothing fancy, I'll just have a tuna sandwich on rye and an ice coffee." Another day, I came back from lunch in the rain to find John in my office at the light table looking at slides with a soggy girl in a raincoat and fishing hat, her eye pressed into a loupe. When she raised her head, I was treated to the million-dollar smile of Julia Roberts. Life at *George* was surreal.

Of course, the real work started at night, when everyone could finally concentrate. There was a feeling in the air that you'd miss something if you went home, so nobody did. Nothing mattered to the staff except the magazine. Marriages were breaking up, no one returned calls from their families, and people smoked packs of cigarettes a day. For forty-two consecutive days, we *lived George*.

My original team was made up of my old pal and loyal number two at Hachette, Michelle Tessler, and a photo editor named Bridget Cox. I filled in the rest of the team with freelancers, mostly old friends I knew would be discreet about what they were working on. For the second issue, my friend Laura Forde, a dead ringer for the *Addams Family*–era Christina Ricci but adult-size and a great graphic designer from my *Elle* days, joined my team. Laura was good-natured about taking on the tedious design challenges of the more complicated pages of the magazine. The work required patience and an editor's eye to make it cohesive and stylish at the same time. For weeks on end Laura was trapped in her cubicle, working intensely long hours.

The staff often worked until eleven at night doing the nut-and-bolts work of the magazine, which was often impossible to concentrate on during the day with the phones ringing off the hook. At eight o'clock somebody would order dinner from one of the local restaurants, often from John's favorite, a tiny Brazilian restaurant on Ninth Avenue called Rice and Beans. One night, the managing editor unpacked the bag of food from Rice and Beans, setting containers on a large table. She walked over to Laura's cubical and put her vegetarian Feijoada on her desk. Laura looked up from her work and, at the sight of the take-out container, lost it: "Can I at least get the tiniest bit of exercise and walk over to pick up my meal from the table?" John and I roared with laughter as Laura ranted on, "I mean, I feel like I'm a veal calf in a feeding pen with people plunking food down in front of me all day and I can't move!" A few days later, John left an envelope on her desk with a gift certificate for a meal for two at Nobu in Tribeca with a note that said, "Even veal need to eat, go out and get a great meal on me at Nobu."

Laura always made me laugh. A couple of years later, she was the first person to explain to me what email was. I didn't understand what she was talking about, so she simplified it: "Matt, email is perfect for you. You can cancel things without calling someone or worrying that they're going to pick up the phone."

Once, Carolyn set up camp on the couch in my office. After a few minutes of chatting, feigning shyness, she said, "Honey, can you go get me some pizza? I don't want to have to talk to all those kids out there." I walked out to a makeshift buffet next to the printers and carried two Cokes and two slices of pizza back to my office. John walked in and asked Carolyn, "What do you think of the magazine?" He was trying to be cool, but I heard trepidation in his voice. Her mouth full of pizza, Carolyn assured him, "John, it's exactly what it *should* be."

To this day, I'm awed at how emphatically the twenty-eight-year-old Carolyn was able to put things in perspective. She always made me feel good about what I was doing, and when she showed up at the office, I felt like someone had my back. She didn't know so much about politics either, but when she looked at the work and gave her approval, it was with such confidence that it always sounded like I'd found the perfect solution.

The magazine was falling into place nicely, but the most pressing problem was that we still didn't know what *George*'s first cover would be. Walking to my office after lunch, John came toward me in the hallway. He playfully wrestled me against the wall and said, "What are you doing tonight?" Things were so intense at the office in those days that I never made any plans. He released me and said, as I tucked my shirt back in, "Herb Ritts is in town, he's a friend, and we're going to talk about the cover." How could I impress Herb Ritts, who'd shot a million magazine covers and had twenty-five coffee table books in every bookstore? "Come over at eight or so," John said, walking away.

I arrived at John's house way too early and circled the block to kill some time. After a few laps, I rang his buzzer. "Herb? Matt? I can't hear you." John's voice echoed out onto North Moore Street. I shouted, "It's Matt," and heard the front door unlatch. Inside the apartment, I looked around and was relieved that it wasn't lavish or pretentious; in fact, my friends at *Elle Decor* would have probably thought it was awful. It was the entire floor of the building, with north- and south-facing views and great proportions. The renovation had been done before Carolyn had come into the picture, and it seemed as though the architect had probably taken John to the cleaners, installing fancy wood finishes, granite counters, and complicated track lighting. It was very '80s. Carolyn attempted to warm the place up with girly things like throws from ABC Carpet and the like.

John offered me a Rolling Rock. I sat down and tried to look comfortable. Carolyn sprawled next to me, putting her arm on the back of the sofa behind my head. She stared at me with her clear blue eyes. "Matt, where did you grow up? I bet Connecticut." I mentally examined myself, searching for clues to her comment. *Was my sport coat too preppy? Did I have a bad haircut? Do I have an accent?* Then I remembered that she had grown up one town away from where I had; she was from Greenwich and probably recognized the type.

Herb arrived and John introduced me. Herb was warm and friendly, and I liked him immediately. I complimented him on his latest book. I was feeling *a little* insecure, as usual. Was he wondering why John had hired me? Was he being sent in to size me up? He turned out to be a nice and attentive man, who would become another support system for me.

John led us to a nondescript local restaurant, not exactly a health food place but almost. I stared at my menu, wanting to make the right choice in front of my famous dinner mates. Herb glanced over at me and said, "Matt's looking for the burger." Again, my insecurities kicked in. *Does he think I'm a 'hamburger type'? Is this menu really cool and I don't know it?* Reexamining the menu, I realized Herb was probably looking for the burger too.

We started firing off ideas about who should be on the cover.

Within five minutes, we'd mentioned every celebrity in Holly-wood. We knew the person had to be an American; apple pie with an edge. John suggested President Clinton, but that seemed too obvious. Herb said, "How about Cindy?" Not being on a first-name basis with *any* celebrities except the ones at the table, I wasn't sure who he meant. Carolyn jumped in, "Cindy Crawford's perfect. She's all-American, a self-made woman, sexy, strong, and smart." Carolyn's infectious enthusiasm carried the day.

Now that we'd agreed on our first choice for the cover, we needed a concept for Cindy. I described an Alberto Vargas drawing from the 1940s of a seductive, half-dressed girl in 1776 regalia. Then Herb suggested dressing Cindy as the magazine's namesake himself. John loved the idea of illustrating the theme of *politics as pop culture* using a pop culture figure like Cindy. So Herb called Cindy at home from the restaurant to ask her if she'd be interested. It was as simple as that.

At the office the next day there was no second-guessing our decision; the level of talent John was able to corral for our cover was more than anyone at Hachette could have dreamt of. Our new vision of the country's first president was about to get as much attention as our famous editor.

4.

LADIES AND GENTLEMEN, MEET *GEORGE!*

I was feeling anxious. The truth was, this cover would be the first photo shoot I'd ever directed myself. John probably assumed I'd done this sort of thing a million times before, so I played the role and began to prepare the call sheet, which lists everyone involved in the production, with my photo editor, Bridget, and faxed it to all the people involved. Neither of us had done a call sheet before, and we wanted to look like pros. George *Magazine, Issue #1 Cover, July 15, 1995, Smashbox Studios, Culver City, CA. Photographer: Herb Ritts. Creative Director: Matt Berman. Model: Cindy Crawford. Hair: Oribe. . . .*

I imagined each of our famous collaborators receiving the fax and thinking, "Who the hell is *Matt Berman?*" Herb was shooting beautiful videos like "Wicked Game" with Chris Isaak and Helena

Christensen at the time, in addition to the photography for which he was famous. Cuban-born Oribe had a credit in every major magazine, with unforgettable cover shots of Christy Turlington, Linda Evangelista, and Claudia Schiffer. And Cindy Crawford was already a household name.

As I sat there at my desk drafting the call sheet for the cover shoot, I somehow snapped out of my insecure funk. *I* was the one working beside the star of all stars—JFK Jr. He could have hired any creative director in the world, but he chose me. I didn't have to explain myself to anyone; I could just let them wonder where I came from instead. Still, I was uncomfortable. As the shoot date loomed closer, I asked John if he was planning on coming with me. I'd feel so much more confident barreling through the door with him at my side.

John assured me, "You're going to be great. Relax and have fun." He handed me a letter to give to Cindy, written on his cream-colored Crane's stationery. In the center of the envelope he'd written, "Ms. Crawford," and in the bottom right corner, in smaller writing, "Kindness of Matt Berman."

I boarded the noon flight to Los Angeles. Looking out of the window, I thought about how far I'd come from Mrs. Clamage's garage. I thought about all those Charlie Nobodies in Stamford who had teased me, and how the most glamorous couple in the world thought I was fine as I was. Beginning to doze, I looked down at the little houses, streets, and farms and thought about how everyone down there knew who John Kennedy Jr. was. I was in a good place—I felt lucky.

I arrived and picked up my rental car. I drove off in a giant beige Buick, finally maneuvering it into the Chateau Marmont's curving, narrow driveway and nearly scraping the sides of the ivy-covered stucco walls. From the expression on the face of the aspiring actor-valet opening my door, I realized that driving an undesirable car in Los Angeles was unbelievably embarrassing, like walking into a restaurant in New York wearing a cheap overcoat or bad shoes.

I grabbed a Perrier from the minibar in my room and walked onto the terrace to get some sun. I'd become so pale from the long hours at work that my office buddies, Hugo and Manny, told me I looked like "toe jam." I looked down at the courtyard and watched the fit, tanned guests chat on cell phones and eat their salads. I made my own phone calls to John and RoseMarie and went to bed, not realizing that I was about to take part in making one of the most talked-about magazine covers of all time.

THE SHOOT

CINDY CRAWFORD

Jet lag woke me up way too early, and I went down to the court-yard to have a coffee, hoping that I looked like the people I'd seen the day before. I found myself wishing I had a cell phone, but even John didn't have one yet; a Sony Discman was about as high tech as it got in 1995. It's hard to imagine now being that *unplugged.*

I chugged down La Cienega Boulevard in the Buick, follow-ing my xeroxed directions to Smashbox Studios, where I pulled my loser boat into a space between a cool '70s Camaro and a Range Rover. Thank God it was early enough that no one would see me getting out of my car.

At the reception desk, a pretty girl pointed me toward the Softbox studio. I found a cavernous space, empty except for an old guy sweeping the floor. I went back to reception and sat there waiting like I was at the dentist's office. Time crawled. Eventually people began pulling up in jazzy cars. Herb drove a black 1960s convertible. He walked through the front door dressed for an outdoor lunch with friends.

"Hey, Matt," he said. "What are you doing out here?" Swoop-ing me up, he said, "Let's go see if anyone's in the studio." I chuckled and said, "I think it's just a guy with a broom."

Herb's assistants started hanging the backdrop, a gray piece of paper. The stylist unpacked racks of clothes. Oribe set up his combs, scissors, and spray bottles in front of a mirror and took a white powdered wig that he had borrowed from the Metropolitan Opera out of a box while Carol, the makeup artist, laid out her palettes and brushes.

Finally, Cindy Crawford arrived, looking more beautiful than in photographs, soft and delicate. She asked the question of the day: "Is John coming?" Herb answered comically, "No, but we've got *Matt*!" Cindy glanced at me with the look of a game show contestant who'd picked the wrong curtain and ended up with a year's supply of detergent. In consolation, I handed her the note John had entrusted me to deliver. She brightened after reading it and asked me how long I'd be in Los Angeles and what my plans were. I told her, "Today is my big plan." She laughed, making me feel comfortable at last. The day was starting to be fun.

Everyone gathered around a table to look at photocopied images of paintings of George Washington when we noticed something common in all of them. When Kate Harrington, the stylist, saw it, she burst out laughing. Apparently, the general is often depicted with a huge bulge between his legs. Herb asked me what I thought of the idea of stuffing a sock down Cindy's pants. John didn't mind a little shock value, but I didn't feel that *chicks with dicks* was what he had in mind. Herb said, "Let's do it and we can always take it out later." I knew John would think it was totally gross, but I rolled with it.

Cindy walked onto the set and took a heroic stance in front of the simple backdrop. Each pose was punctuated by Herb's "That's great! That's great!" Every so often Cindy loosened her body, rotated her shoulders, rubbed her legs, and resumed her posing. Yet nothing looked quite right. The Revolutionary War–era coats Kate had rented from Western Costume, a Hollywood institution for film costumers, looked like leftovers from a bad TV miniseries and Cindy, in her white wig, looked like a granny. After an hour of Oribe combing and shaping the wig, we found a solution that resembled George Washington but made Cindy look pretty and feminine. Kate mixed combinations of coats and Lycra sportswear until Cindy looked enough like our Founding Father, but sexy. Once we got the look down, Herb rapidly shot a few rolls of film and said, "I think I got it."

Having seen how great the Polaroids of the image turned out, I agreed that we were ready to wrap. The bulge in her pants wasn't a battle worth fighting and would be easy to retouch. Photo shoots are so different today; with digital photography, everyone can see the actual final image and know the result instantly. When a good photographer, model, hairdresser, and makeup artist are booked, very little can go wrong. I don't care if you shoot in front of the Taj Mahal; if you don't have the talent, the shoot will be bad. Having worked with this level of talent from the word *go*, the standard was set for the next twenty years of my career.

I wasn't free yet. Kate piped up, "Group picture! Group picture!" Herb's assistant got behind the camera. Herb, Kate, Carol, and Oribe formed a conga line behind Cindy. This was the kind of stuff I made fun of at the office and was too self-conscious to participate in, so I hoped to be overlooked. But Herb yelled out, "The creative director, we need our creative director!" I pretended that I needed to make an urgent phone call and signaled for them to go ahead without me. The heckling I'd receive from everyone at the office for participating in a conga line would be too horrible; I couldn't do it.

There was a flurry of air kisses as everyone said their good-byes. I hung back, wanting to be the last to leave so nobody would see my *old man* car. I flew back to New York, where my staff and the editors were putting the final touches on the layouts.

I spent the next week planning the next issue with my staff. Unlike today, when you can easily search for photos on the web or choose images from Corbis online, we had to fill out request forms for what we needed and fax them to Getty Images or the Bettmann Archive. Days later, huge piles of slides and stills would arrive. John loved to edit film with me, sorting through the piles to find images for each page. He would inevitably choose the most obvious picture in the pile. His instincts were to publish familiar images that the reader would automatically respond to, but I liked to use less obvious ones. I'd imitate John making a "John Kennedy photo request" by flailing my hands around, almost spitting with enthusiasm as I said, "I'm thinking of this picture of a woman, very glamorous, in a white dress, and it's blowing up with a gust of wind from the subway." Before the laughs died down, I'd continue, "You know what would be great? I know this photo of this couple, maybe it's a sailor and a nurse, making out in Times Square." John would just walk out of the art room, shaking his head.

About a week after the cover shoot, I received a FedEx package from Herb's studio. I took the box into my office and shut the door. Inside was a thick pile of contact sheets with X's in red grease pencil by some images, circles around others, and stars and circles around others. I brought John into my office and waited for a reaction. The whole thing could have backfired if Cindy hadn't looked gorgeous, but I was pretty sure he'd be pleased, because she looked like George Washington but was beautiful. He was thrilled. And then his attention went right to Cindy's groin.

"Maestro, what the fuck?"

I assured him the bulge was removable. Michelle scanned the contact sheets, and we tried different shots with a *George* logo over each one. John handed me a yellow legal pad with his cover lines scribbled onto it, and the cover started to take shape.

John looked at the final layout and was irritated that the *I*'s of the words *Inaugural Issue* didn't have serifs. It was a sans serif font, Antique Olive, almost sacred in Paris because it is the beloved logotype of Air France. I had gotten my way with so many bigger things that I agreed to customize the *I*'s and draw serifs on them. I thought no one would notice, but Jean-Louis saw the change with a glance. "Matt, you have completely destroyed the integrity of the font." I knew that Jean-Louis was right, but John had signed off on so many of my ideas that I felt it was a very small price to pay to make him comfortable.

John, Michael, and Jean-Louis approved the cover design. I sat with Michelle to perfect the details. Michelle zoomed in on the image to check a measurement, and Cindy's face filled an oversized monitor. "Wow," I said to Michelle, "this really looks like *something.*"

I flew from New York to the printer's in St. Louis. I had hoped John would come, but he opted out. John wasn't a micromanager, like so many people I've worked with over the years. I was beginning to learn that his deciding to hire me meant he trusted me unconditionally with all aspects of the job. Conceptualizing expensive photo shoots, representing the magazine by appearing on monthly segments of entertainment news shows, and overseeing the printing of two million copies of the biggest launch in magazine history, I recognized that John had confidence in me that I didn't have in myself. With each event, I learned he was right to trust me, and I began to trust my own instincts. It was all working.

In the printer's linoleum-floored reception room, fluorescent lights buzzed overhead, the vending machines had hamburgers in them, and tables were set up in a U shape. There were all kinds of baked goods arranged on different styles of plates, like at a school bake sale. Overhead hung a big banner that read *Congratulations George #1.* It was one of my many experiences of the *Oh, they thought John was coming* syndrome.

The owner of the printing company said a few nice words, then handed me a plaque with the cover lacquered onto it, with my name and the date engraved on a brass plate. There was a plaque for John as well. There was a Midwestern sincerity and sweetness about the whole thing that I found touching until my cynicism kicked in. I wanted to call John to have a laugh about the ceremony, but once I walked into the huge and noisy press-room and saw the miles of paper soaring high into the air, with recurring blurry images of Cindy Crawford flickering by at sixty miles an hour, I wished John had been there to share the moment with me. I spent a few days watching giant Midwesterners take stacks of *George* pages off the press for me to proof for color. I flew back to New York with the first bound issues and our plaques in the overhead bin.

Boxes of the magazine were delivered to the office, and we treasured them like gold. The staff got *one* magazine each, and Rose kept the rest under lock and key. We stood around in groups, slowly turning the pages. The magazine hit all of the marks because it was commercial, featured a big star, and it was a fun take on politics. It not only looked right; it *felt* historic, glossy, and heavy, at nearly three hundred pages. Many of the editors saw the initial images of the Cindy cover and tried to talk John out of it, saying it was inappropriate or stupid. As usual, John stuck to his guns and stood by Herb's work and mine. I was proud of our work, but I was so close to the story that I didn't understand *how* big a deal it was. News stories and gossip columns reminded us that the whole world was waiting to see it.

I put my copy of *George* into a white envelope and was about to head home around 7:00 p.m. when the phone rang. "Hey, Little Buddy, where are we going for dinner tonight? Aunt Jane's hungry!" Jane Hsiang, my old *Elle* pal, lived on Sutton Place across town, and we often had last-minute dinners together during the week. Jane liked spicy food, so we'd go to Rosa Mexicana or Korea Palace near her place. When I told her I had the first *George* in my bag, Jane raised the bar to Da Silvano so we could have some fun. She knew the media crowd at the restaurant would die to get a glimpse of the magazine.

Inside the restaurant, Jane gave me the highlights of the O. J. Simpson trial that she'd been watching all day on television, then reached across the table and took the magazine from me. Although she had seen it in the taxi, she acted as though she was laying eyes on it for the first time, gasping, "Oh, Little Buddy, this is *fabulous*!" She slowly flipped through it for a few seconds and held the layouts clearly exposed for onlookers to see. When she felt enough eyes were peeking at the cover, she slammed it closed and pressed it into her lap. Her hands covering the image, she said, "You know something, Little Buddy, you are going to be a *very* big art director. This is a *very* big deal!" I tried hard not to laugh, and I nodded as Jane looked at me with exaggerated seriousness. As she held the cover out and rubbed her hand on the shiny surface, a man dining beside her leaned back in his chair and almost fell over trying to sneak a peek. Jane snapped, "May I help you?" He stammered, "I just wanted to . . ." Jane cut him off with a dismissive chuckle and an eye roll.

The next day, there was a 9:00 a.m. press conference to unveil the magazine at Federal Hall, a historic building on Wall Street where George Washington himself once spoke, and maybe even slept. I had been so isolated, working late at the office and limiting my social circle to people involved in the magazine, that as I walked down Nassau Street and saw all the news vans with satellite dishes on top, I wondered what was going on. I was still a bit clueless about the publicity a Kennedy could generate.

I walked into the throng of reporters, and someone ushered me to the front row of the auditorium. Aunt Jane was right; this *was* a really big deal. I wished that someone had involved me in the production of the unveiling. I would have lined the entry with models from Cindy's agency dressed in the same George Washington costume, drumming on Revolutionary War drums or forming an archway of crossed swords. Instead, John ended his speech with "Ladies and gentlemen, meet *George!*" and twirled a lame light box around to reveal the cover. I wanted red, white, and blue velvet bunting falling away to reveal the cover, and a fife-and-drum corps playing, and maybe those old-school camera flashbulbs exploding. Cheesy or not, *George* was launched to a round of applause and news coverage in every language around the globe. Little Buddy was suddenly a *very* big art director.

5.

WHO'S TIGER WOODS?

"What are you doing tomorrow morning?" John asked late one Friday afternoon as we were preparing the second issue of the magazine. I shrugged my shoulders. "Come to a screening of the new Scorsese movie with me," he said, slinging his backpack over his shoulder. We agreed to meet at 9:00 a.m. sharp on the Upper East Side. There went my sleep-in.

John had recently met with Robert De Niro at his restaurant, Tribeca Grill, and had asked him to be on the cover of the second issue of *George*. The response had been so strong to the Cindy Crawford cover, with news channels and newspapers all over the world reprinting the image, that we'd decided to continue disguising other stars as George Washington and ride the momentum. De Niro had agreed to the request as long as John saw his new movie and found a way to promote it on the cover.

I stood on a corner near Park Avenue, watching every approaching car for John. Finally I heard the rapid ticking of a bicycle chain, and he appeared right beside me. I wondered why he hadn't taken a cab. Observing John patiently fastening his bike to a pole with his lock, I thought maybe it was the solitude, speed, and general anonymity of getting around on two wheels that was most appealing to him. We rode the elevator to the tenth floor, and John tapped lightly on the glass of a locked office door. After a moment, a little man came toward us with a big smile, then knelt down and wrestled with a key at the bottom of the big glass door. When he stood up and opened the door, I realized it was Martin Scorsese. He patted each of our backs as we walked in, talking in his trademark rapid-fire manner. "Hello, guys, good morning, nice to meet you, come in, come in." I felt like I was visiting an uncle I hadn't seen in years.

Mr. Scorsese told us we were about to see a rough cut of *Casino*, a movie about Las Vegas starring Sharon Stone, Joe Pesci, and Robert De Niro. He led us into a plush screening room and left. The lights went out, and the voice-over began, *"In Vegas, everybody's gotta watch everybody else."* Five minutes into the movie, I heard snoring, looked over, and saw John, *People* magazine's Sexiest Man Alive, with his head back, mouth open, dead asleep. I hoped Mr. Scorsese couldn't see him.

Jacqueline Kennedy and John, 1962.

My mom and me in 1968.

*Although our mothers were worlds apart, they taught us both
to try to fit in despite our unusual childhoods.*

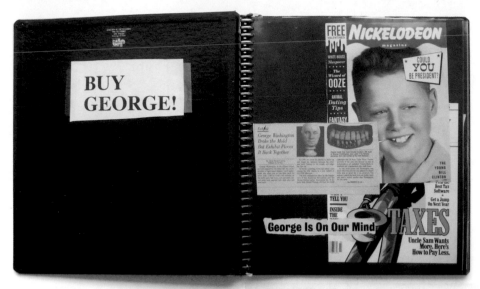

The scrapbook with inspiration for George magazine that John gave me the day I met him.

John posing as Adam "nude" (in his briefs on my office floor) to accompany our September 1997 cover of Kate Moss as Eve.

Art school days, me on the roof at Parsons, 1984.

DEC 1995

December 1995, George hits the newsstands (above).

DON'T SIT UNDER THE APPLE TREE

've learned a lot about temptation recently. But that doesn't make me desire any less. If anything, to be reminded of the possible perils of succumbing to what's forbidden only makes it more alluring. But while I'm playing Hamlet with my willpower (Should there's always the distraction of gawking at the t who simply couldn't resist. We can all gather, like u tch those poor souls who took a chance on fanta y-handed—to remind ourselves to keep to the safe article I just read gave a name to the kind of tem it's not a striking body or a pile of money or a n more intangible. It's the inevitable by-product of

My Hachette ID from my Elle days.

George

John's and my first crack at a cover idea over too many beers: Cindy Crawford covered in one-dollar bills—we nixed it because it looked too much like a financial magazine (left).

A pinup drawing by Alberto Vargas that inspired issue number one of George.

Our second choice for the cover marked up for retouching by Herb Ritts . . . note the bulge in Cindy's pants (below).

X JK
MB.

The label from the package containing the cover film sent from Herb's office (below).

HERB RITTS STUDIO
1106 NORTH HUDSON 2ND FLOOR
LOS ANGELES, CALIFORNIA 90038

Matt Beaman
George Magazine
4122
1633 Broadway
NYC NY 10019

(212)767-5532

Spectragraphic, Inc.
Quality Control
View With 5000 Kelvin Only

Cover sketches.

Robert De Niro holding a Kennedy heirloom, George Washington's actual sword (below).

CHEAP THRILLS
35 FREE SUMMER ADVENTURES COURTESY OF GOOD OL' UNCLE SAM
JENNY McCARTHY ON DON KING, BORIS YELTSIN & PAMELA ANDERSON LEE
AN INTERVIEW BY JOHN KENNEDY

George

not just politics as usual..

THE YEAR IN POLITICS

NORMAN MAILER
ON THE REAL REASON WHY CLINTON WON

POLITICAL PREDICTIONS
FROM THE EXPERTS: DICK MORRIS TO AL FRANKEN

YOU PICK THE BEST & WORST OF '96

HOTTEST TV TALKER
COKIE ROBERTS
MOUTHS OFF TO JOHN KENNEDY

ELECTION YEARBOOK: PHOTOS FROM THE TRENCHES

INSIDER'S GUIDE
TO INAUGURAL MADNESS

WHAT YOU NEED TO KNOW ABOUT WELFARE

JANUARY 1997
USA $2.95 CANADA $3.95 UK £2.50

We painted stars and stripes directly on Jenny McCarthy's tongue (above).

Claudia Schiffer wearing no costume at all (left).

George
NOT JUST POLITICS AS USUAL...

A painting by Lucas Cranach the Younger, reference for our Garden of Eden cover (right).

George
not just politics as usual...

Happy Birthday, Mr. President
By Letty Cottin Pogrebin

Kate Moss as Eve with real plants and live animals (above).

Drew Barrymore posing as Marilyn Monroe for our September 1996 cover.

George's version of a political cartoon: my sketch for a spoof on a campaign idea.

George Tames's famous photograph of President Kennedy in the Oval Office, entitled "The Loneliest Job."

A sexy version of "The Loneliest Job."

The Monica Lewinsky scandal with a twist, a female president and young male intern, shot by Ellen von Unwerth.

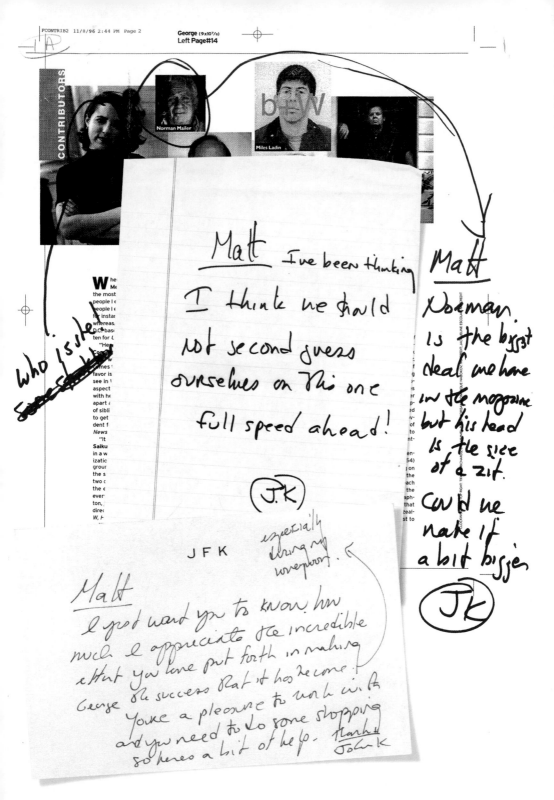

Various notes from John. He always used his sense of humor to motivate.

George

John Kennedy
Co-Founder
Editor-In-Chief

November 8, 1996

To: All
From: John

Just to let you all know, the late nights are not for naught. We've just learned that the Nixon cover is a 40% sell-through so far and rising. Given that it was a black and white and a pick-up shot, we should be pleased.

Soon, Matt Berman will be able to sit bare-bottomed on the Xerox machine, put it on the cover and we'll be assured of a sell-out.

Thanks.

John hamming it up in the George *art room.*

John loved editing film with me, especially all of the historical photo research.

I was envious of how free John felt. If he was tired, he nodded off. If he was anxious, he left work and went to the gym. If he was hungry, he helped himself to fruit from the desk of my deputy, Michelle, delighting the Jewish mamma in her. "Take some little plums, John, the season is a minute long."

I loved the movie but had a rough time watching some parts. I looked away during the scene when Joe Pesci says, "Listen to me, Anthony, I got your head in a fuckin' vise. I'm gonna squash your fuckin' head like a grapefruit if you don't give me a name." He then proceeded to do just that. This was a rough cut, pre-edit, pre-censoring, and the character Tony Dogs's eyes popped completely out of his head. I looked over to see John waking up, hands over his face, saying groggily, "Gross!"

The De Niro cover would be the first *George* shoot I would handle completely on my own. The Cindy Crawford cover was great, but Herb shot it in the same style he would have employed for *Vanity Fair*—gray background, classic studio lighting, and a rented Revolutionary War jacket. Once again I thought of the star British photographer Nick Knight, whose images I had used for the prototype; if he shot the cover, it would be truly different. I called Nick and explained who I was and what the magazine was. Once I told him the subject was Robert De Niro, he was in.

We agreed to promote *Casino* on the cover, but the image of De Niro needed to be a *George* cover foremost. The fact that I could even think that way showed the progress we had very quickly made in establishing our own look. I hired an amazing stylist named Paul Sinclaire, who had an impeccably tailored, navy George Washington coat made in London, which he paired with a monochromatic combination of a hot pink Gucci shirt and silk tie in a '70s style to give De Niro the period look of the costume design in Scorsese's film. This would be De Niro's wardrobe.

John invited me over to his house the night before the shoot. When I got there, he handed me a Rolling Rock, and I waited while he went into another room. He came out and handed me a long, dark leather box. "Here it is." Inside the box was a beautiful, heavy, polished sword.

"It looks like a real George Washington sword," I said, turning it to catch the light. John laughed. "That's exactly whose it was." His father had been given the sword during his presidency. John couldn't remember the occasion or who had given it to JFK, but it was the real thing. I carefully slid it gently back into its velvet-lined box and snapped it shut. "What if I leave it in the cab?" John shook his head and rolled his eyes. "You won't."

The next day, De Niro strutted around the studio in full regalia, hamming it up, sword in hand. "You know, you really look like George Washington," I said. De Niro walked past me regally and said, "I *am* George Washington." Between De Niro's professionalism, Nick Knight's skill behind the camera, and Paul Sinclaire's discerning eye for style, our second shoot went off without a hitch. Though it had a completely different feel from the first cover, the shot of De Niro spearing an ace of spades with Washington's sword for the second issue of *George* turned out to be an equally arresting image on the newsstand.

I had photocopies of every American archetype that I could think of to suggest to the celebrities we shot. We researched which stars had upcoming movies that coincided with our publication date, then we contacted their publicists. Often, *Vanity Fair* or *Vogue* had gotten to them first, but we had our pick of the leftovers. As each cover hit the newsstands, there was so much hoopla that we were challenged to outdo ourselves every month. We chased down stars to sit for covers wherever they were. We once flew to Costa Rica with a giant pair of feathery wings borrowed from *Angels in America* for Woody Harrelson to wear to illustrate a cover story about religion. Once we locked down the dates for the talent, their agents would inevitably ask, "What do you think you will do on the cover?" I'd reach for my stack of references and rattle off a few concepts. A lot of these ideas were produced as *George* covers, but some never made it, including the Statue of Liberty, Uncle Sam, Rosie the Riveter, Andrew Jackson, FDR, the Iwo Jima Memorial, and Benjamin Franklin.

I always wanted to do a cover of the painting *American Gothic* by Grant Wood. After star couples such as Bruce Willis and Demi Moore turned it down, I approached John. "What if you and Carolyn pose on the cover as *American Gothic*?" John ran his hand through his hair and shook his head. "Oh, right, Matt, like business is *that* bad that I have to whore myself and my wife out on my own magazine cover?"

I still think it would have been amazing: John wearing overalls and staring stone-faced into the camera, Carolyn in a Depression-era housecoat. She usually didn't smile in pictures anyway, and she wore her hair pulled back in almost the same style as the farmer's wife. However, as I got to know John and Carolyn better, I began to understand their sensitivity to the way they were perceived in the public eye, and I really appreciated their need for privacy.

There was something very brotherly about John. Growing up, my brothers, Brad and Andy, had always looked out for me. Now that I had John as my champion, the similarity between him and my older brothers was not lost on me. In the '70s, Brad and Andy attended an uber-preppy school called The King School because my parents thought the public schools in Stamford were dangerous. I was reminded of John when I thought about its picturesque campus, with its colonial buildings and playing fields, the Jew-fros, penny loafers, and J. Press oxford shirts. I never felt comfortable in a prep-school atmosphere, but my familiarity with that lifestyle put me at ease around people like John and the editors at *George.*

At Christmastime, John personally picked out a gift for every staff member. We gathered in his office as he gave a juicing machine to Jen, the vegetarian, a Dunhill lighter to the English editor who smoked like a chimney. Hermès scarves, Mont Blanc pens, and Knicks tickets were given to others. John handed me a large, gift-wrapped rectangle. When I unwrapped it, I found an original print of a 1950s stripper in gold body paint by the photographer Weegee. I was floored; I'd seen and admired this image in books and couldn't believe that John had actually bought it for me. I loved it. Later that evening Carolyn warned me, "You better like that thing; we almost had to mortgage the house for it!" Rose later told me that Carolyn had told her, "I want Matt Berman to open his present in front of the whole staff so they see that John takes him seriously."

John respected me, but plenty of others didn't. In one design critic's review of the layout of the first issue, he looked at it from the viewpoint of a typography geek and completely missed the unique way we handled the photography, as well as the coolness of our unpretentious design. When I did layouts at *Elle,* Régis, my first boss, would say, "Just lay the type down casually, like you don't care." He knew that typography that was too crafted in a self-conscious and labored way looked nerdy, and *Elle* was about being cool.

I read the review to John. It ended obnoxiously with " . . . in the end a design must be suited to its purpose, and by that criterion Hachette creative director Matt Berman has done an admirable job. *George* looks the way it has to look. Unfortunately, the way it has to look is embarrassing." John cut me off mid-paragraph, "What an asshole! Who the hell is he, anyway?" As usual, John was unconditionally on my side.

For every naysayer, there were thousands of others who spoke highly of our covers. *Vanity Fair* published a Barry Blitt cartoon with has-beens and undesirable stars wearing wigs on *George* covers. We loved the attention. One night I met a *Vanity Fair* editor at Balthazar and he asked me what future covers we were planning. I naively told him that we had every American icon from Paul Revere to Mickey Mouse in mind. Touching my arm, the editor told me, "I have a fantastic idea." He put one finger in the air dramatically and said, "Adolf Hitler." I gave him a mock-hostile eye roll and smirk. "That's *some* American icon!" The next morning, I told the story to John, and he laughed. "Oh, brilliant. They'd *love* that over at *Vanity Fair*. 'John Kennedy put Hitler on the cover of *George*.' In a Jewish city like New York on top of everything!" I couldn't decide if the competition was trying to feed two novices a catastrophic idea or if it was simply an attempt at humor.

There was so much talk about every move we made, both bad and good, that it was impossible for me to enjoy the success of *George* as it happened. I heard negative comments louder than positive ones, and I was so green at thirty years old that I thought people were out to sabotage me, criticize me, or discover that I didn't know what I was doing. I never allowed myself to expect too much. I didn't want to jinx a good thing, and I was waiting for a brick to fall on my head at any moment. When I told people where I worked, I wasn't sure if they envied me, admired me, or wanted me to crash and burn. As *George* staffers, we all experienced on a small scale the schadenfreude that John experienced his entire life.

John taught me a trick to use whenever a star was hesitant to commit or wasn't interested in our suggestions for their cover shoot. "Matt, call them back and tell them we understand, and '*maybe next time.*'" I reminded him that we didn't have a backup and were already behind schedule. John assured me, "We'll just hold on to our balls and see if they come around." It was a good lesson in negotiation and power. John's rule was: *If you want an answer right now, the answer is no. If you wait, we'll see.* If all of that didn't work, a call from John would seal the deal.

My time at *George* was star-studded. We all became experts in celebrity behavior and loved witnessing the fireworks (or fizzle) between John and the superstars of the day. One Monday morning, RoseMarie stopped John and me in the hallway and said, "Don't forget, Demi Moore is coming to the office at eleven to talk about her cover." John called a meeting to go over our strategy. Wanting to top her two *Vanity Fair* covers—one in which she is wearing a painted-on man's suit and the other of her pregnant and nude—we thought up other risqué ideas for Demi: Demi as Vargas girl or Demi as a seductive Statue of Liberty in see-through chiffon draping. After an hour of arguing, we decided we wanted to shoot her as a sexy Martha Washington half dressed in bloomers and a corset.

When Demi arrived, John came out of his office to get me. After Cindy Crawford and Robert De Niro, we'd chosen Howard Stern and Charles Barkley dressed in Revolutionary War coats for the next two covers. Although those shoots went smoothly,

John knew how awkward I still felt around celebrities, so he tried a sink-or-swim tactic. Putting his hands on my shoulders, he said, "I've got to go upstairs for a few minutes. Go into my office and introduce yourself." I walked to John's office and peered through the doorway. I saw Demi with her hands clasped behind her back, examining the trinkets and photographs in John's bookcase. With the midday sun coming through the windows, she was more beautiful than I expected; delicate bones, flawless skin, and straight dark brown hair swept away from her face and clipped casually in the back. Her hands were henna-tattooed with a Hindu design.

I took a breath and walked in. "Hi, I'm Matt, John's creative director." She turned around, put her illustrated hand out, and said in her famous raspy voice, "Hi, nice to meet you. Demi." Everyone in the whole world had been calling her "Demmy" Moore, but she'd just pronounced it "De-*meee*," which sounded much more like the way a Frenchman would pronounce the word *half* as in *demitasse*. I repeated her name in my mind a few times. We talked about the view as, one by one, the men of *George* found an excuse to come into the room, all of them saying, "Nice to meet you, Demmy." More of them than usual had taken an interest in this cover. She was wearing jeans, a T-shirt, and a tiny lavender cashmere cardigan, stretched tightly around her upper body and fastened with one tiny pearl button right between her breasts. That button was now the focus of the meeting.

John returned to his office and broke the silence by telling her our ideas for the cover. She listened politely, then told us *her* idea of how to shoot her as Martha Washington. After describing her extensive doll collection to the now catatonic men surrounding her, she suggested that she be portrayed as an old-fashioned, porcelain-doll version of Martha Washington. And to be sure the reader knew she was Martha Washington, the doll Demi Moore would be manipulating a tiny George Washington marionette on a string. We all nodded in agreement, as if pulled by strings ourselves, as if her idea was brilliant. So much for "It's our cover."

After everyone else left the room, it was up to me to work out the details of the shoot with Demi. She gave me the contact numbers of her assistant, the photographer she liked, her personal seamstress, and an artist from whom she had once bought a doll that could serve as the perfect model for the photo. I wrote everything down, sure that this would be the last time I would be in contact with her until the day of the shoot.

Early the next morning, a Saturday, the phone rang at my apartment. Figuring it was my mother calling to see if I was still alive, I let the machine answer. "Hi, Matt? It's Demi." The husky voice continued, "If you're home, pick up." I grabbed the receiver with a curt "Hello," trying to sound like I'd just run in from somewhere. She asked, "Did you get hold of Nancy, my friend who makes the dolls, yet?" This lady was running the whole show, but since she was a big star, we all just kind of rolled with it.

THE SHOOT

DEMI MOORE

We shot Demi's cover in the same Los Angeles studio where we'd shot Cindy Crawford's. I soon discovered that our *George* doll cover would become part of a growing *oeuvre* of creepy photographs of Demi portraying various dolls. She showed me photo after photo from her collection: Demi jammed in a corner as a lifeless, freckle-faced Raggedy Ann wearing red-and-white striped hose, Demi as a nineteenth-century china doll, and the most disturbing, Demi in a giant cardboard Barbie package staring expressionless through the life-size cellophane window. It made me wonder if she didn't feel *real,* or like a shell of a person filled with some synthetic stuff.

The scene got stranger; Demi insisted on her bosom being body-painted with red-and-white stripes to create a bodice. Knowing this had been done twice for *Vanity Fair,* I found it embarrassing. As the makeup artist went to work on Demi's chest, the phone rang. It was John calling to make his apologies for not coming. I handed the phone to Demi. When she was done talking to John, I took the phone, glad to hear a familiar voice. "What's goin' on out there, Maestro?" I described the scene to John in a whisper, making him laugh. "I wish you could see what I'm looking at now—she's nude from the waist up with her arms in the air while this guy is painting her tits in red and white stripes." John cracked up. "Oh, Jesus! This cover's gonna be a doozie."

When the images of Demi came back, they were passable, but the lighting was flat. In order to fit the entire crazy puppet concept on the cover, the image had to be small, and Demi's head was the size of a quarter. Nobody was thrilled with the images; they didn't read as "Martha Washington" at all. The whole concept was convoluted, and I was bummed that we'd given in to her every step of the way.

A few weeks later, my assistant, Stephanie, came into my office, squirming. "Demi Moore is on the phone, and she sounds sort of mad," she said. I picked up the phone. "Hi, Demi, how are you?" The angry, raspy voice snapped back, "Not so good. I just got a copy of the magazine." I started to feel annoyed; we'd done *everything* she'd wanted, and *she* was mad? Then I tried a new tactic. "Oh, man, I don't know what to tell John," I said, exhaling. "I'd tell him how angry you are, but he *really* loves the cover." *That* changed her tone. Softening up, she said, "Oh, I didn't say I *hated* the cover, I just said I looked a little bit red." I was learning how to navigate the terrain. It was the first of many times in my life when I used John's psychology to sort out a problem. Even today, when a touchy issue comes up at work, I ask myself, *What would John do?* I often find my solution. Recently a bully at work was causing trouble, and I heard John's voice in my head, *"Just shine a bright light on them and they squirm."* Today, each time I lock horns with a bully, the JFK Jr. bright light trick works every time.

While I loved my growing friendship with John, I missed the cozy familiarity of my old life at Hachette and looked forward to Jean-Louis's weekly dinners with editors. Most weeks, Jean-Louis's secretary, Jacqueline, would call a group of editors and give them the address of a restaurant, usually Remi, on West Fifty-third Street. The food was good, and it was located halfway between the office and J.L.'s apartment in Museum Tower. Jean-Louis would reserve table number one, the large round one in the center of the room, because it encouraged an informal, relaxed atmosphere.

My regular seat was between two of my favorite ladies: Marian McEvoy and Jean-Louis's wife, Barbara Cady. Barbara was a statuesque blonde from the Midwest who had been, among many other things, the editor of *Playgirl* magazine in the 1970s. She loved to laugh, and after a cocktail, which she ordered as soon as the maître d' seated her, there was no telling what would happen. She looked as pretty as Shirley Jones, but when she got to talking about sex, publishing, or politics, she was more a combination of Gloria Steinem and Erica Jong. Marian and Barbara were about the same age but from different planets. I would imagine them back in the 1970s: Marian riding through Paris on the back of a Vespa in head-to-toe Yves Saint Laurent; Barbara leaning over a light table, choosing a *Playgirl* centerfold, wearing white cashmere, with Burt Bacharach music playing in the background. They both had great senses of humor.

One evening, Jean-Louis invited the new editor of one of Hachette's magazines into the circle. The editor was ambitious and saw the evening as an opportunity to talk shop and impress J.L. I cringed as he bored the table with long stories about what he was planning for his magazine and how he was going to "boost readership." I'd had my share of dinners with French bosses during my *Elle* days, and I knew that this line of conversation wasn't going to cut it. He was seated next to Barbara, and each time he brought up the name of someone in publishing, he would pause and explain to Barbara who he was talking about and where they worked. "Barbara, Anna Wintour is the editor-in-chief of *Vogue*" or "Graydon Carter is the editor of *Vanity Fair*."

I could feel the tension radiate from Barbara, who the editor was treating like the boss's dumb blonde wife. He continued to prattle on about "the bottom line" and "appealing to his demographic." In the middle of one of his sentences, he touched Barbara's arm lightly and said, "Barbara, Tina Brown is the editor of *The New Yorker.*" The fuse was lit. Barbara slammed both palms down on the table, rattling the dishes. "Will someone tell this *jerk* that I'm not a moron?" She began grabbing tableware in front of her, mimicking, "Barbara, this is a wineglass." Raising her voice, she continued, "Barbara, this is a fork!" Marian and I tried holding back our laughter by pressing each other's legs under the table so hard that I thought we'd bruise each other. "Barbara, this is a salt shaker!" She reached for the sugar bowl, when Jean-Louis, holding back a smile, attempted to calm her rage, saying, "Bar-bar-a, Bar-bar-a, calm down, Bar-bar-a, please." I looked across the table at the editor and his wife, who were frozen and stunned. They'd probably never seen anything like that before, but it was episodes like these that made me love Barbara.

My all-time favorite blonde was still always Carolyn, and her visits to my office were a welcome distraction. By this point, she'd become Mrs. Kennedy and would often stop by the *George* office after lunch with John, looking to play. I liked to think that it was my charismatic charm that lured her into my office, but it might also have had something to do with the stacks of new photography books from the Strand or the piles of European fashion magazines all over my coffee table. My subscription to *Hello!* was a bonus.

Carolyn would slip into my office and shut the door, her white-blonde hair pulled back tightly in a bun. "What are you doin'?" she'd ask. Before I could answer, she'd throw her coat and giant Hermès handbag into a corner and make herself comfortable on the sofa. Flipping through the new Italian *Vogue,* fumbling in her bag for a cigarette, she'd settle in: "Honey, you got some matches around here? Oh my God, is that Amber? She looks *gorgeous*!" In two minutes, she'd make it through half the magazines in my office, letting them drop all around her as she finished with them. "Hand me that Helmut Newton book. Honey, do you have a Coke or something?" Having grown up with two much older brothers, I was an expert at entertaining girlfriends.

Carolyn spotted *People*'s "Best and Worst Dressed" issue and rifled through it. Stopping at a picture of a Hollywood star in her forties, we examined it and concluded with simultaneous nods that she was definitely over the hill. Carolyn turned to me with a look of terror on her face. "Do you think that's going to happen to me?" Knowing the hard truth that none of us, not even Carolyn, is immune to the aging process, I blithely lied: "Nah, not you."

Having transformed the space from an art director's office into a girl's college dorm room, every surface littered with magazines and books, overloaded ashtrays, and empty soda cans, Carolyn was ready to have a real chat. "Honey, what's the matter?" I'd rev myself up and launch into a tirade about everything that had happened since I'd last seen her. She'd ask about everything going on in my life and listen to all of it, smiling when I told her what was really pissing me off, cutting in here and there with "He's such a psycho!" or "You're *still* talking about her? Why haven't you fired her already?" Always on my side, just like John was.

Carolyn and I shared a similar dark and sarcastic sense of humor. She understood why I always felt down on the first sunny day of spring when everyone else was lunching in the sun and skateboarding down the sidewalks, or why a rainy day gave me a lift. "What's going on with Bitter Seth?" she would ask, referring to my dry-witted cousin in San Francisco, who I spoke with almost every night. Seth and I recognized each other as the two black sheep of the family and grew close because of it. We both have a skeptical view of the world and a love of irreverence. Seth hated his nickname, but I explained to him that it was a compliment; most other nicknames Carolyn bestowed were linked with four-letter words. He should have felt honored.

Carolyn was my protector, always smoothing out bumps in the road, whether they were social or work-related. When John and I didn't communicate, Carolyn would interpret for us. One day, John said, "I want to see a stupid movie tonight with Matt Berman." I ignored him, thinking he was trying to do something nice because I had put in so many late nights. An hour later he stuck his head into my office and said, "You know, we should go get a beer after work and hang out." I gave a halfhearted smile and nodded, thinking that he would forget about the invitation by the end of the day.

Then Carolyn called me. "What's wrong with you, Matt Berman?" Carolyn always called me *Matt Berman,* like it was a one-word name. "John's been asking you all day to go to a movie or grab a beer, and he thinks you're a little stuck-up asshole and don't want to go with him."

"What? That's crazy! I thought the big star wanted to take poor Matt out for a beer because he worked so hard."

Carolyn sighed. "Honey, get over yourself. He just wants to hang out with you. He *likes* you."

I didn't believe her; I thought that he was just trying to be nice. I often find making plans with people a burden, and I assumed he must have felt the same. The very idea that he genuinely wanted to hang out with me socially was unfathomable.

I knew I made John laugh, but I also felt like the opposite of his *real* friends: jocks who he'd play football with in the park. As the years went on, I realized John understood me and accepted my eccentricities. One time, John was in a group of the guy editors in the hallway talking about Tiger Woods, who had won the 1997 Masters. I stood by and listened to everyone reliving each moment of his amazing performance in the tournament.

During a lull in the conversation I tapped John on the shoulder. "Hey, John, who's Tiger Woods?"

"Who's Tiger Woods?" Gary asked. Rich threw his hands up. "You're kidding, right?" I shook my head side to side. Hugo, laughing, said, "Come on, seriously?"

They all looked toward John, who pressed his palms outward to quiet the chatter. "I think it's amazing that Matt doesn't know who Tiger Woods is." The guys looked at John, perplexed. "That means, in 1997, in the twentieth century, it's clear that Matt Berman did not read a newspaper, turn on the television or a radio in a week's time." Then, trapping me in a mock headlock, he laughed, "That's incredible!"

Although I didn't know much about current events, no one hesitated to ask me about the hottest places in town. My brother Andy was looking for a cool new restaurant, and I suggested one that Carolyn's friend owned in Tribeca called Independent. The next day, Carolyn ran into my office and put her palm flat onto my chest. "Honey, you're going to kill me." She sat down and stuck a Marlboro Light between her lips. "John and I were at Independent last night, and this strange couple kept staring at us from across the room." I imagined how irritating and disturbing that must have been. Carolyn fired up the Marlboro Light and took a drag. "I was getting more and more freaked out, and then they got up and started walking toward us!" She took another drag and continued, "So I was giving them the dirtiest *get the fuck outta here* look, staring daggers at them, and the guy walked right up to us, stuck out his hand, and said, 'Hi, I'm Andy Berman. I'm Matt Berman's brother.' Honey, I almost died."

RoseMarie entered the room packing her own box of Marlboro Lights. John had gone off to a meeting, and she needed to decompress. After telling her about my brother, Carolyn launched into some *extremely* intense girl talk with Rose. I tuned them out, they were babbling on about boys and clothes. Then Rose looked at Carolyn with a childlike smile on her face. In her best kindergarten teacher tone she said, "You're all signed up for your *group* ice-climbing class in New Hampshire this weekend." Carolyn mashed out her cigarette, muttering, "Oh, great weekend. He goes off with his buddies, and I'm stuck in a stupid class with strangers."

I said, "I'm going to keep all my shades down, order in, and watch *Back to School* with Rodney Dangerfield for the millionth time." Carolyn turned to Rose and said, "I should have married Matt Berman." I knew what she meant; John's social, sport-filled weekends always sounded like too much work to me.

Carolyn was exciting to me because she looked so *exotic,* with her full lips, white hair, and azure eyes, yet she came from a normal suburban family like I did. I can picture her sitting on a bar stool at Odeon, rumbling with laughter, then stopping me mid-sentence to carefully remove an eyelash from my cheek with her pinky. She was glamorous, and protected and empowered me.

Just as my office had become Carolyn's refuge, my hideout was in the office of the publisher, Elinore Carmody. Elinore had also worked for Hachette prior to *George.* She was a little older than me and helped me navigate tough situations. She looked like a pretty Greenwich WASP, but in fact she had grown up in a tough Irish neighborhood in Queens. She reminded me of the badass girls I knew in high school who smoked in the parking lot and cut classes. They always seemed more mature and more interesting than the preppy girls or the boring smart Jewish girls.

Elinore and I complained and whined so much that Hugo Lindgren, who was then a junior editor at *George,* nicknamed us Bittaman (*bitter man*) and Bittaqueen (*bitter queen*). Elinore embraced the titles, and to this day she signs emails to me *HRH Bittaqueen,* or simply *BQ.* "Bittaman, what's happening to you happened to me," she'd say as she lit a cigarette. "I used to be the cute, funny protégé too"—she blew smoke upward—"Now we have a lot of pressure." Bittaqueen knew how to play the corporate game and how to have the most fun doing it. When I told her I was flying back and forth to Los Angeles for cover shoots, she stopped me midthought. "Bittaman, I'm going to tell you how to do it. You go a day early to *prepare,* and sit by the pool. Then, when the shoot is over, you stay a day later to *edit,* and sit by the pool. I mean, why are you killing yourself?" I didn't have the nerve to do it then, but I can't say I haven't tried it in recent years. When I did something that showed I was taking her advice, she'd lean back in her chair and maniacally imitate Mr. Burns from *The Simpsons,* saying, "Exxxxcellent." Apparently, I was catching on.

The next time I flew to Los Angeles, I managed to squeeze two cover shoots into one weekend: one of Barbra Streisand, the other of Drew Barrymore. John was going to join me for the Streisand shoot on Saturday, and I'd handle Drew Barrymore myself on Sunday. When we landed in L.A., the plan was for me to call Barbra's assistant, Kim, and arrange a time to meet at Barbra's house to discuss the details of the shoot.

Rose and I had been dealing with Kim all week. She was difficult, but we held our tongues. I called at 4:00 p.m. to ask about meeting with Barbra. "She's editing her movie and we can't do it till later," Kim told me. I called at 6:00 p.m. "She's still working," Kim snapped, with no apology for keeping us waiting. John called my room and asked, "Maestro, what's going on?" I told him

Barbra was editing and didn't want us to go over yet. Finally, Kim called at 7:00 p.m. "She's ready."

John and I got into our rented convertible and pulled onto the Pacific Coast Highway. He pointed to the right at a mansion high on a bluff. "You ever been to the Getty?" I shook my head silently. "What's the matter?" John shouted into the wind. "I'm nervous," I told him and gave him a terrified look. "We're going to see your uncle Morty's idol! Relax, after a few minutes she'll be like your Aunt Barbra."

6.

MARTY, WHAT ARE YA THINKIN'?

We pulled up to the mammoth wooden gates of Barbra's house. There didn't seem to be a button for guests or an intercom box anywhere, so John got out of the car and shouted into the trees, "Hello? Anybody home?" We heard the click of a latch releasing, and the gate opened automatically.

Situated high on a cliff overlooking the Pacific, the house was huge and designed to feel like an idyllic American home, with picket fences, pointed gables, and bright white clapboard siding. There was a meandering flagstone path leading to an arched front entrance, where I saw a tiny, pale figure in the doorway. Carolyn's warning, "She'll eat you alive," echoed in my head. As we walked down the path, John whispered, "Remember, we have dinner plans at nine o'clock." He wanted to be sure he didn't get tied up all night.

Funny Girl was leaning against the doorframe with her arms folded and a familiar, wry, half-smile on her face. "John, what a young staff you have," she said in her best Dolly Levi voice. She was wearing white cotton from head to toe, a pair of stretchy pants, and a sort of *Flashdance*-style off-the-shoulder top. She was dewy and freshly moisturized, her hair artfully mussed. She looked so perfectly casual that it must have taken some time to achieve the look. I had the feeling she hadn't been editing a movie all afternoon.

I always loved *What's Up, Doc?* and *The Owl and the Pussycat* when they were on television, and I always defended *Guilty,* the album she did with Barry Gibb, to all my music-snob friends. I saw *The Way We Were* with my parents at the Ridgeway Theater, and my dad told me not to laugh at my mom when she cried at the end. I had rented all of her movies the week before in New York—*all* of them, even *Yentl* and *Nuts*. There was no mistaking who was standing in front of us, but her features seemed to be a miniature version of Barbra Streisand. Her eyes were cooler, fox-like and piercing, not the loveable eye-rolling Fanny Brice I was hoping for. She looked really good at fifty-five years old. John kissed her on the cheek and introduced me. After shaking hands and exchanging pleasantries, she offered us a tour of her house. She spoke in a dramatic way, emphasizing every syllable and punctuating occasionally with a Brooklyn-inflected "You know what I mean?"

The house was traditional in style but Hollywood in proportion. It was filled with colonial-style antiques and folk art, with girly touches here and there. There was an antique teddy bear sitting on a lace doily on a spooled rocker. She summed up her style emphatically. "I just like *American* things." Sunlight streamed into massive rooms packed with treasures. In the dining room she stopped and flashed a finger over her shoulder at a huge painting. "Hey, John, you know what *that* is? It's a *Hopper*," she said, strongly emphasizing the *H*.

She led us into a surprisingly humble kitchen, leaned casually on the counter, and offered us both something to drink. I remembered some advice that John had given me about running off at the mouth when I was nervous. "Don't feel like you have to say something, Matt. Be *mysterious*; let people wonder." At this point, I was being *extremely* mysterious. Her maid brought us giant glass tumblers filled with soda, and then put a plate filled with spring rolls on the counter. They were arranged in a circle, with dipping sauce in the middle. Barbra took one and nibbled at it, saying, "These are wonderful. I love them so much that my chef in New York FedExes them out here."

After our snack we went into a formal living room, which had a sprawling pink carpet. "It's beautiful," I said. "It's an *Aubusson*," she replied quickly. Then John chimed in, "Yeah, it's beautiful." She gushed with meticulous detail about how it was silk and from France. She rattled off its dimensions and its age.

We took a step forward. "Hey, hey, hey, guys!" Barbra exclaimed, lunging forward, hand outstretched. "Could you walk around it?"

"You want us to take our shoes off?" John asked.

She put two fingers to her lips and nodded up and down like a little girl. Now we each had an oversized glass tumbler in our hand and sock feet. The floor was slippery, and I was sure I was going to trip and ruin the Aubusson.

We followed her upstairs to the bedroom. It was flowery and covered in chintz. Piles of fancy pillows on the bed, a chaise longue by a huge window overlooking the ocean, and, like in every movie star's house, a bureau cluttered with silver frames containing pictures of herself along with other famous faces. I spotted one that I really wanted John to see. It was a photo of Streisand shaking hands with President Kennedy. I worked up my courage and said, more to John than to her, "That's a great photograph. Maybe we can use that on the editor's letter page."

Barbra sniffed, "That is something very personal and important to me. I can't have it printed in the magazine for the whole world to see." I looked at John and mouthed, *What a bitch*. John, pushing his hands downward, signaled me to *calm down*.

Noticing that the swimming pool was just below her bedroom terrace, John joked, "Hey, Barbra, do you dive from here into the water in the morning?" She laughed, throwing her head back theatrically. Barbra leaned on the railing and cuddled herself in the evening air, rubbing her upper arms with her long-nailed fingers. It was dusk, the sky was getting dark, and you could see the lights of Santa Monica twinkling on the horizon. The view was spectacular. "It's a pretty spot, isn't it, John?" she dreamily mused. Then she glazed over and stared at the sunset. Transfixed by the view, Barbra said, "The sky's so pretty, not gray, not pink. I love colors that you"—she dramatically paused here—"can't quite define." Then she turned her head quickly toward John and said, "You know what I mean?"

We followed her back downstairs and she pointed out more *objets* on the way. I was hoping we would get to the work part soon, and I increasingly felt like a third wheel on a blind date. We slipped down a hallway in our socks, still holding our soda tumblers, and stopped at a fish tank that was built into the wall. This was more John's speed, and it inspired him to say, "Great fish tank!" She squatted down next to it and opened some paneled cabinetry under the tank. A little staircase popped out so that children could step up to see the fish.

"That's neat," John said. She looked over her shoulder and said, "It's called good design."

We ended up in some sort of den or sitting room and were, apparently, finally going to talk about the shoot. She took a position dead center on a colonial sofa that had probably been owned by Paul Revere. She tucked her knees under her chin, making herself very small and cozy. "What time are we starting?" she asked. Here was something I could confidently answer. "Kim and I thought it would be good to set up at 9:00 a.m."

"Well, that's a very bad plan," she answered, drawing out the *a* in *plan*. She then informed me how *she* envisioned the day ahead of us. Then she changed the subject. "You boys hungry?" John, feigning disappointment, said, "We have a dinner to go to at nine." Barbra responded, "Well, I've eaten already. Where are you going?" she asked. "The Buffalo Club," John said. I looked at him, thinking, *Where'd you come up with* that *one?* "Fun," she said. At that point, Barbra became very hostess-like, standing formally beside the door. John leaned in and kissed her cheek. I opted for a handshake, then awkwardly put my left hand over both of hers, for some reason. "Good-bye," she said, smiling.

We pulled out of her street onto the highway, and I could finally relax—for about ten minutes. Then what I thought was going to be a quiet dinner with John and maybe his cousin Bobby Shriver turned into a star-studded night in a crowded booth with Arnold Schwarzenegger, Maria Shriver, Tony Danza, and Chazz Palminteri. It was like the opening of a Planet Hollywood.

This was one of the times when I was John's wingman but wished I'd been back at the hotel. There weren't enough seats at the table, so I got wedged between Russell Simmons and a starlet I didn't know then and haven't heard about since. John and I were seated at opposite ends of the table, and seeing how uncomfortable I was, he called out, "Hey, Russell, tell Matt about *your* magazine." Simmons was publishing a magazine called *One-world* in addition to his myriad other projects, and John thought we could talk shop. The waitress came to take our orders, and Russell told me to get the chicken pot pie, which was apparently famous there. Someone poured me a glass of champagne, and I started to feel more comfortable. I chatted with Russell about how I was looking to buy an apartment in New York, and he said he had one for sale that I should look at. I replied, "That sounds cool." I was just being polite, but I was thinking, *This guy thinks I'm rich. How could I afford his place?* As if sensing my apprehension, Russell explained that while he had a huge apartment in NoHo, the apartment he was thinking about for me had been used as a screening room and was eleven hundred square feet, which sounded more like it. He told me to have John call his office in the morning and he'd give us the details. John called, and agreed to do an interview for *Oneworld* and before I knew it, I was a homeowner.

After the dinner, John and I went back to Shutters, where I plopped down on the bed and stared at the ceiling, going over the day in my head. I had felt out of place at the dinner table, but then I thought about all of Carolyn's pep talks. *I* was the one who'd come with JFK Jr. and was the creative director of the hottest magazine around. Who were half those people, anyway?

The next morning I woke up early with that sickening first-day-of-school feeling in anticipation of the photo shoot. I called

John's room, and he told me to call him just before I went down for breakfast so that he wouldn't be hassled while standing alone in the lobby. At breakfast John ordered oatmeal with fruit, and I copied him. "Maybe we should go in two cars," John suggested, slurping his coffee. He was going to ditch me at Funny Girl's at some point during the day. I ran up to the front desk to sort that out, trying not to leave John unprotected at our table for too long. The car rental process took a good twenty minutes. Back downstairs I found John sitting staring straight ahead with his hands in his lap, food in front of him, waiting for me to begin eating. Now I always think of John when I see someone begin to eat before the rest of the table is served. John's manners remain the gold standard in my mind.

We were off to Malibu for The Main Event. John pulled onto the freeway and I followed, in a blue version of his red convertible. He took his sunglasses off and waved them in the air, mouthing, *Don't you have sunglasses?* I, of course, didn't. I tailed John's car closely, certain that he would arrive at Barbra's gate first and I would be trapped on the other side trying to explain to a voice on the hidden intercom that I was *with* Mr. Kennedy and not some psycho trying to get inside.

THE SHOOT

BARBRA STREISAND

Once inside the gate, we realized there was a photo shoot going on that we knew nothing about. Without telling us, Barbra had agreed to an *InStyle* magazine shoot the same morning as ours and had "forgotten" to mention it. A black velvet backdrop stood right in the driveway. Barbra was in a dark décolletage evening gown and high heels, standing with her legs shoulder width apart, fists planted firmly on her hips. She was looking straight at the camera, with the look of a snarling tigress on her face and a ferocious mane of hair. I nudged John and whispered, "It's going to be a loooong day!" John clapped his hands together and cracked up.

As soon as that shoot wrapped, the crew began dismantling the set in the driveway. Ours was next. Barbra walked toward us, glamorously fluffing her hair and carrying her heels as if in between takes on a movie set. She seemed very serious as we began to plan the shot for the *George* cover.

The shoot was elaborate. We'd hired the costume people who had done the gowns for *Dangerous Liaisons,* and we'd gathered flags, thimbles, threads, pincushions, and fabric stars as props for Barbra's transformation into Betsy Ross. Debating possible background choices, we looked at cloth backdrops that the photographer had brought. One was authentic for the period but dull and brownish. However, it was pure Americana, and I knew Barbra would love it. John and I thought that it was boring for the cover, but we figured we'd zap in a more colorful one on the computer later.

We still needed an appropriate throne for our seamstress. I remembered that the "Paul Revere" sofa inside was upholstered in a rich red that would photograph well, *and* I figured using it would please her. Barbra fanned her nails out on either side of her head and asked, "Should I crimp my hair?" I wasn't sure, but I thought crimping was something from the '70s, more *Love Boat* than Liberty Bell. I knew John would be no help on this. To keep things rolling, I said that I thought it was a good idea.

We set up the shot in a small guesthouse, where Barbra edited her movies. It was the original house that was on the property. The photographer and his assistants, the hair, make-up, and prop people, stylists, publicist Ken Sunshine, manager Marty Erlichman, Kim the assistant, John, and I all crowded into the room. "What exactly are you editing in here?" John asked, gesturing at the equipment.

"It's called *The Mirror Has . . .*"—she paused here, raised an eyebrow, and continued—"*Two Faces.*"

Barbra wriggled into lots of different poses on the Revere sofa. Watching her move as the camera flashed furiously, it became apparent to me why she was a star. It was impossible to take your eyes off her. She saucily pulled her skirt up to display her garters and bloomers. She coyly pulled fabric stars from her cleavage, saying, "Oy, what are these doing here?" Next, she cut some stray threads with her teeth. "Oh, that's *some* thread!" Then she took one long stitch through the flag, flashed a long-awaited Fanny Brice smile, and said, "*This* is going to be one *hell* of a flag, boys!"

We heard chuckling from the back of the room. It was Erlichman, Barbra's manager of thirty years, with his tinted glasses. Barbra's expression took on that dreamy trance again. "Marty," she said, "what are ya thinkin'?" "What am I thinkin'?" he answered, sounding like the counterman at the Carnegie Deli. "I'm thinkin' this is the way you started; silly stuff, costumes, funny hats." Barbra chuckled. Marty had been with her since she was eighteen years old and knew how to make her feel comfortable.

We had the cover shot, but we decided to shoot more film just to be safe. Barbra started clowning again for the camera. And then, all of a sudden, the curtain came down as her demeanor changed. Her eyes went foxlike again. Aiming her polished pointer finger at three chattering assistants, she sternly demanded, "You, you, and you, you're in my line of sight, I need this set clear!" The three victims scurried out as if they had wet the Aubusson. Distractions gone, Barbra resumed her vaudeville act, picking imaginary lint off her bosom, "Oy, got to send this to the cleaners!" Adjusting her bodice, "Don't tell *Mr.* Ross." Pretending to prick her finger, "DOC-TAH!" She was camping it up, and like so many stars, she was at her best when the cameras were rolling.

When we finished the shoot, John pecked Barbra on the cheek, thanked every single person in the room, and peeled out in his convertible. I lingered to look at some Polaroids, arrange for the film to be sent to New York, and wrap things up. I drove back to Shutters, slightly shell-shocked. John had left a note at the front desk. "Good-bye, Dolly! Great job, see you at the office."

A week later a package with a Malibu return address arrived for me at the office. Could it be a thank-you? I reached in and pulled out the picture of Barbra with President Kennedy, along with a note asking whether we needed it for the story. I waved it in front of John's face as he was talking on the phone. He hung up the receiver, looked at me in mock horror, and said, "This is very personal to me. I don't want this published for the whole world to see!" We printed it.

A couple of years ago, I got an email from Biz Mitchell, who was the editor of *George* at the time of the Barbra cover. She attached the cover image from the book *My Passion for Design* by Barbra Streisand and wrote one line: "It's called good design."

John flew back to New York on Saturday, and I checked out of Shutters and into the Chateau Marmont, where I would stay until Monday. After two long days at Barbra Streisand's house, I was looking forward to having time off between her cover shoot and Drew Barrymore's, which we would be shooting the next day. I loved Los Angeles but never had time to sightsee; my trips were limited to a triangle between LAX, a hotel, and a photo studio. Since I had a free afternoon, I called Elizabeth Kaye, one of the writers for *George*. Elizabeth decided to show me the Los Angeles of her childhood. Her family owned Botany 500, the men's clothing company that had been popular in the 1950s, '60s, and '70s. Credits on television programs like *The Dick Van Dyke Show* and *Get Smart* included the tagline "Wardrobe by Botany 500."

We started the day in Hollywood, driving past the Paramount studio gate, the quaint Charlie Chaplin cottages on Formosa Avenue, and the building where 1940s hot spot Ciro's had been. I was disappointed to see it had been replaced by The Comedy Store. We had lunch at the Farmers Market and drove down Rossmore Avenue past the Ravenswood apartment house, once the home of Mae West. As I looked at the building, I thought about the autographed photo she'd sent me years before and imagined her sitting up there in her crazy all-white Louis XIV-furnished apartment. Elizabeth told me she and her sister were visiting a friend in the Ravenswood when they were teenagers in the '70s and ran into Mae herself in the elevator. "What did you say?" I asked. Elizabeth laughed, "We were speechless. We couldn't get any words out, so we both *bowed,* and Mae nodded."

We drove high into Beachwood Canyon to see the Hollywood sign, then cut across the city on Mulholland Drive and down toward Brentwood and Topanga Canyon. Elizabeth pointed out where Streisand had lived with Jon Peters in the '70s. We both agreed she must have been cooler then. We ended up in a Malibu bar at sunset, drinking beer, eating peanuts, and throwing the shells into the Pacific. Having grown up around New York, I was programmed to criticize Los Angeles: *There's no culture, the people are fake,* and *they have earthquakes.* The truth was that Los Angeles was a magical place, where so much of what I'd obsessed about growing up had been created, and I loved it.

THE SHOOT

DREW BARRYMORE

The concept for the Drew Barrymore cover was to celebrate Bill Clinton's fiftieth birthday by featuring Drew as Marilyn Monroe circa 1962, when she sang "Happy Birthday" to President Kennedy at Madison Square Garden. Back at the hotel after my day with Elizabeth, I called the photographer Mario Sorrenti, who came down to the garden accompanied by Frank, a childhood friend of his turned makeup artist, and two assistants; Lars and another one he called Sauce. Mario's casual style and confidence were refreshing. He came from the fashion world and had become a star photographer after shooting beautiful black-and-white photos of his former girlfriend, Kate Moss, for Calvin Klein's perfume Obsession. He was handsome, spoke two languages, and was the son of an Italian artist and a bohemian American mother. Mario had a pure talent to be able to pick up a camera and take the most amazing photographs effortlessly.

While I was talking, Mario looked down at one of his assistant's feet and said, "Dude, did you shave your toes?" We all looked down at the stubble and doubled over laughing. This was going to be very different from the shoot at Barbra's. I told Mario that my first idea was to have Drew as Marilyn at a podium with a microphone, like at the real event, but I worried that the podium would eat up too much of the cover and read as a big boring block. Mario looked pensive, so I added, "If the podium is too much, we can just use the microphone." Mario stopped me. "Dude, what's a podium?" I must have seemed wound up and said *podium* so many times that it sounded abstract, because someone offered me a puff of a joint, and Mario added, "Dude, relax, it's going to look like Marilyn." Even today, when we're working together, Mario laughs about how neurotic I can be.

The next day we drove to Smashbox Studios for the shoot. I gave the makeup artist a copy of Norman Mailer's *Marilyn*. It had a close-up of Marilyn on the cover, shot by Bert Stern, and you could really see what was going on with her makeup. I took one last look at the dress the stylist had made, a replica of the nude sequined dress by the designer Jean Louis that Marilyn had worn. I must have been driving everyone crazy, obsessing about every detail, because someone gave me another hit of a joint as we sat and waited.

Drew walked in right on time with a small entourage of her

young staff and no publicist. She was exactly how I had hoped: pretty, sweet, gracious, and full of charm. With a big smile, she grabbed my forearms with both hands and told me she'd been watching Marilyn Monroe movies for days. She had such an infectious excitement and enthusiasm for doing a *George* cover that it made me think that maybe this was the secret to success in general: Do every job well and take each one seriously, no matter how big or small.

Mario wasn't so enthusiastic. He seemed upset about lighting and technical issues, and I heard him say, "Fuck it then, we'll use natural light." I imagined the worst: The shoot was going to be a disaster, with Drew Barrymore looking like a homeless woman in a wig or an amateurish cover with a local model dressed as Marilyn for a film festival article. I think it was the pot; I was becoming paranoid. After Herb Ritts with his fifteen assistants and the Cecil B. DeMille production at Barbra's, I was concerned about Mario, Frank, Lars, Sauce, and this *natural light* situation.

Drew walked out of the makeup room looking amazing. I told her so, and she whispered back, "Thank you." Once she slipped into our fake Jean Louis dress, she sat up in a certain way and posed and positioned herself until it really felt like we were looking at Marilyn Monroe.

This would become the first of many magic Mario moments. He positioned Drew in front of a black velvet background next to a window and snapped a Polaroid. He rubbed it in his hands and blew on it, then peeled the backing to reveal a velvety, moody take on Marilyn. Mario laughed with pleasure as we marveled at his first try. After a few rolls of real film, Mario tried Drew against a white background. He peeled back the paper to reveal the most ethereal Marilyn I'd ever seen. With no stress, in three hours we did a cover that was much more beautiful than Barbra Streisand's or Demi Moore's. Those covers were so overcooked by the actresses' micromanaging them that they looked canned. Helmut Newton says in his biography that you always have to leave a few things unplanned on a shoot to allow something spontaneous to happen, which is the difference between a good photo and a really great one. Drew trusted our concept and had faith in Mario, so the results were infinitely better.

I flew back on Monday alone, no fawning stewardesses and no paparazzi waiting for me at Kennedy airport. When I returned to the office on Monday, feeling great about Drew's cover shoot, I was immediately met with a growing scandal over my expense report. Don Piccolino, a pocket-sized accounting guy, had gone over my report from California and decided that four hundred dollars a night at Shutters in Santa Monica was too extravagant. He'd picked the wrong moment to get into it with me. I was wiped out from the traveling. I'd returned with two major Hollywood cover shoots and was irritated by the pettiness of his nickel-and-diming. I forwarded Piccolino's memo to John, who wrote a response to Don that began, "I gather there was an issue over where Matt and I stayed during the cover shoots for Barbra Streisand and Drew Barrymore. Personally, I found it quite private, and that's one of the reasons I suggested we stay there."

The whole thing was small-time and silly, and John knew it. But it still pissed me off. The job and all of the personalities were hard to wrangle. I wasn't extravagantly paid and worked long hours without question. The last thing I needed was to be nit-picked over a hotel bill.

My inability to move on when something upset me made John laugh; he loved situations that sent me into one of my tailspins, and he was milking this one for all it was worth. His teasing persisted for weeks as I cursed out Don Piccolino, calling him Nick Nack after Hervé Villechaize's character from *The Man with the Golden Gun.*

After work one night, I went home and kicked off my shoes. I pressed Play on my answering machine to hear a familiar, nasal voice say, "Hi, Matt, it's Don Piccolino. I'm sorry to bother you at home, but I've been looking a little further at this expense report, and I see a glass of orange juice for twelve dollars." I was fuming as I listened to this jackass. "Matt, you just can't call up and book these toney hotels at the drop of a hat." The veins were popping out of my head as I reached for the receiver to call Rose and tell her what was happening when the nasal voice lowered a bit, and lowered again, then morphed into, "Matt, it's John, call me back."

The answering machine beeped a second time, followed by the message "Hi, it's your mother, just call me and tell me you're alive." *Guilt trip.* My mom was right, though; I was blowing off my family, and I needed to make time for my parents, brothers, and cousins. It was hard to enjoy normal life when things were so exciting, intense, and full of surprises at work. I was a star at Hachette, weekends visiting the family for a graduation party or holiday dinner felt like trips to another planet and stirred up old memories that I wanted to forget. I preferred it when my family could visit me in New York.

One Friday night, my younger cousin Scot, a corporate lawyer from Connecticut, came in to the city to meet me for dinner. With John and Carolyn living in Tribeca, the neighborhood was an exciting place to go out. Leftovers from the '80s, like Odeon and El Teddy's, were still popular, but my favorite was an Italian restaurant called Barocco on the corner of Church and Walker streets. Scot met me at the restaurant and we sat down and ordered some drinks. He said, "You're never going to believe who just walked in." I turned to see John and Carolyn a few tables away. I walked over to say hello, and John insisted that we join them. This wasn't the evening Scot had had in mind when he left his condo an hour earlier.

Carolyn sized Scot up in one look and took him under her wing; she had a knack for making people comfortable. "Where do you live, honey?"

"I live in Stamford," Scot said.

Carolyn grabbed his arm and clamped it down on the table. "Honey, you've got to move into the city."

"I tell him that once a week, Carolyn," I said, egging her on.

Scot nervously chuckled. "Why?"

"Why?" Carolyn looked at me, exasperated. "Because it's exciting, there are a million things to do, great restaurants."

Scot wasn't convinced. "There are some good places in Connecticut."

Carolyn looked at him in disbelief. "Well, you'll meet more interesting people."

I pointed my thumb at Carolyn and rolled my eyes. "Um, *hello*, Scot."

After dinner Scot and I walked to the West Village. He did most of the talking: "She's so beautiful, but man, what a mouth on her, every other word was *fuck*." I was so used to Carolyn's bawdy language that I didn't realize what a surprise it must have been to someone who only knew her through the tabloids. "I couldn't understand half of what you were saying to each other. Seems like you guys have a lot of private jokes." We went to Caffe Dante on Macdougal Street for dessert.

Sipping my Irish coffee, I asked, "What did you think of *him*?"

"Oh, he was super nice, but Jesus, he was chewing with his mouth open and spitting food everywhere!"

Everyone in my family wanted to meet John, because everyone in the *world* wanted to meet John. I tried to spare him from awkward introductions and made excuses to my relatives. *I'll be working with him for years,* I thought. *Maybe there will be better moments for these meetings in the future.* The only member of my immediate family who had met John was my older brother Andy with his wife, Sabra. They were in town visiting from San Francisco and wanted to see where I worked. I told Andy to come by the office around lunchtime to pick me up, and if John was in, I'd introduce them again.

Andy has always been the big man on campus. In high school,

teachers would say to me, "Wow, you're Andy Berman's brother!" They'd end up disappointed when I sat silently in class, not living up to my brother's charismatic legacy. The truth was, Andy reminded me of John, so I couldn't wait to see B.M.O.C. face-to-face with JFK Jr.

I deposited Andy and my sister-in-law on the couch in my office and went to John's office to ask if he had time to say hi to my brother. John said no problem, then puzzled me by walking off in the opposite direction from my office. He stopped halfway down the hall, made a U-turn, and walked back. As he got closer, I heard him mumbling, "San Francisco, Grateful Dead, Lawyers." Before greeting Andy, John was going over in his head everything I'd ever told him about my brother. I found it sweet the way he did this, always looking for a way to connect with people and make them feel comfortable.

A few weeks later, I found myself on an 11:00 p.m. Air France flight to Paris to shoot a Claudia Schiffer cover. She would be wearing nothing but a blue ribbon with the names of the winners of the 1996 presidential election.

The plane landed around noon the next day. I had a cup of coffee and a croissant as I waited for my bags. As the car service headed for Hôtel Costes, we passed all the places I'd seen in French movies. Having worked for French people for so many years, I felt immediately comfortable in Paris.

The shoot took place prior to the election, so I'd brought with me two versions of the blue ribbon—one for Clinton and one for Dole. I sat next to the beautiful Claudia as she had her hair and makeup done, and she asked me about all the stars we had shot so far. I liked Claudia and was pleasantly surprised to find her so calming and easy to talk to. Claudia was especially interested in Barbra Streisand; she was a big fan and loved *Funny Girl*. She laughed as I gave her a play-by-play of the crazy two days John and I had at Barbra's.

To make Claudia comfortable while undressed, the photographer, Satoshi Saïkusa, had partitioned off an area just big enough for the two of them. He passed me Polaroids of each shot until it read like a perfect campaign-style pinup. The cover turned out almost exactly as I'd sketched it and looked great. This wasn't always the case; covers often evolved during photo shoots and strayed from the original plans—sometimes for the better, sometimes not. When we shot Harrison Ford as Lincoln for the cover, the stylist, Claire Todd, did such an amazing job replicating Lincoln's suit and top hat that I wanted to emphasize the effect by making the magazine cover look truly antique. I borrowed an ornate glass daguerreotype from my antique dealer mom. Our photographer, Stéphane Sednaoui, took a close-up of the daguerreotype's frame and set our portrait of Lincoln inside the frame. The effect was amazing, especially because Mr. Ford insisted on not smiling; either in an effort to stay true to character or out of anger. He was posing in a top hat, shirt, tie, vest, jacket, and boxer shorts. Our seamstress was late delivering his pants that morning.

THE SHOOT

PAMELA ANDERSON OR KATE MOSS?

For our September 1997 cover, John asked me to come up with a cover image for an article listing the twenty most fascinating women in politics. I scanned the faces of the twenty women and thought that most of their faces could have stopped a clock. I suggested we do a beautiful actress as Eve, the first woman. John always loved a cover of a sexy star, and after our austere Harrison Ford as Lincoln cover, it would be a fresh way to start the fall. John suggested Pamela Anderson. "Why not, but let's do it in a way to really surprise people," I said. I sent Mario Sorrenti a photocopy of a moody Rennaissance painting of Eve by Lucas Cranach the Younger. We discussed doing Pamela nude and natural with no makeup, no sexpot hair, in a lush set of foliage with live animals and a snake. He was excited.

Mario's team and I flew out to Los Angeles, and we got a cab to the Chateau Marmont. At the front desk the clerk handed me a note. I opened the envelope and read: *Pamela can't make the shoot tomorrow. We apologize for the inconvenience.* That was *some inconvenience*—about twenty thousand dollars' worth of airfare, hotels, studio rentals, and sets.

"Hey, Mario," I said, my panic rising, "this is crazy; she's canceling on us." We plopped down at a big garden table and ordered drinks. I didn't want to call John without another plan, so I brainstormed with Mario. "Who in Los Angeles can we ask to fill in here?" Mario suggested a few names but no one who would have the impact of a *George* cover subject. "How about Kate Moss?" I asked. Mario and Kate had been together three years earlier, and I knew that they'd remained good friends since they'd stopped dating. "I can call Kate and ask her," Mario said, walking over to the house phone.

I waited at the table with Frank, Lars, and Sauce for the word. Mario returned, laughing. "She'll do it, but she said that since we're making her *sloppy seconds,* she will only do it in New York—she's not flying here." I called John and ran the idea past him. "That's even better, let's do it," he replied. The only problem was that we had to re-create in New York, in just a few days, the Garden of Eden we'd set up at Smashbox, with real trees, live animals, and a snake with a snake wrangler. Don Piccolino, the penny-pinching accounting guy, was going to flip.

A few days later, we had an identical set made at Industria studios in New York. Unlike Claudia, Kate didn't need a partitioned set. She handed her robe to the stylist, walked into our dreamlike garden, and took her position amidst the foliage and live animals as naturally as Eve herself. She curved her body to imitate the pose in the painting and squealed, "The baby deer just licked my hand!" In between takes, I sat with Kate on a sofa and went over a questionnaire John had given me for our "If I Were President" page. There was a subtitle that said, "The Skinny on Kate Moss," and she asked me what it meant. "It's supposed to be a joke because you are so slim," I explained as she stirred her tea. I cracked open a can of soda and poured myself a glass, wondering why she was pretending she didn't understand the pun—I sensed she thought the subtitle was corny and that was her way of letting me know.

The Kate Moss cover turned out to be one of my favorites. The staff started joking about John signing off on all of these covers with nude women on them. John told me that when he'd described the magazine to his ailing mother, she had asked, "John, is it going to be the *Mad* magazine of politics?" That always made us laugh. Evidently, John wasn't the only one who liked nude women on magazine covers: The newsstand sales soared that month.

———————

The celebrities themselves were often as surprising as the covers. We opted for a Thomas Jefferson costume when George Clooney posed in June of 1997. I had coffee early in the morning with him, and his openness reminded me of John. When the hairdresser put the powdered wig on him, he came out of the dressing room saying, "I look like my aunt Rosemary." He sang a little of Rosemary Clooney's hit "Come On-A My House," then looked both ways and said, "Where's my pint of Häagen-Dazs?" That was one of those shoots I'd wished John had been able to join; I think he would have liked Clooney as much as I did.

The biggest sport of all was Jenny McCarthy, who agreed to let us paint an American flag on her tongue. She sat patiently for half an hour while Andrea, a tattoo artist, painted the stars and stripes onto her outthrust tongue and an assistant wiped away her drool with a paper towel. Stéphane Sednaoui, the genius photographer behind Björk's video for "Big Time Sensuality" and The Red Hot Chili Peppers' "Give It Away," gave the covers a surreal spin.

Looking back on all the covers we produced in five years of *George,* I realize that the most beautiful ones were painless to create because they happened organically as a group effort. The more mundane covers were the result of long, painful days of battling egos and mixed goals. Fortunately, those struggles and skirmishes make for some entertaining storytelling.

7.

IT'S *LOVE STORY* DOWN HERE

John and I didn't go out alone together very often, but ever since Carolyn encouraged me to grab a beer with him I always agreed to go when he asked me. One night, we went to Florent in the Meatpacking District. They had a no-reservations policy, and the only free seats, even for JFK Jr., were at the end of the bar, facing the restaurant. I sat on the stool next to him and tried to act as if no one in the place noticed John. I was excited to be one-on-one with him, but I missed having RoseMarie or Carolyn along as a buffer. I couldn't roll my eyes at Carolyn when John said something corny, and I didn't have Rose to cue me up to tell a funny story. There was a kind of awkwardness between us when we were alone outside of work, and I wondered if John was thinking I liked Carolyn and Rose better because we always had big laughs as a group. It wasn't that; it was just that I always think I'm funnier and more entertaining when I can riff off an audience.

We sat on our stools and ordered bottles of Corona. I didn't say anything at first and was sure John was wondering why his bigmouth creative director had nothing to say now. To break the silence, I brought up the movie *Austin Powers*, just out that month. We compared notes on our favorite scenes, and then ordered some mussels to share. After a couple of beers we finally started to relax, and John laughingly told me what he really thought of all the *George* staffers; who had dog breath, who he thought was a phony, which girls he thought were attractive. I asked John about an editor everyone in the office hated, wondering what he'd say, since we were speaking so candidly. Interestingly, John saw everyone's animosity toward the guy as a positive; he told me that on rafting trips there was always one person in the boat who everyone hated. He believed that the mutual hatred brought everyone else in the group closer together.

As we chatted, John told me a long story about the antics of his dog, Friday, to the point where I warned him, "John just don't turn into one of those assholes who likes animals more than people, like Bob Barker, Bridget Bardot, or Hitler." John laughed. "What are you talking about?" I knew I sounded crazy, but my theories always made him laugh, so I continued. I started in about a woman in the office who was always narking on me. I told him, "If I were being hidden in Anne Frank's secret annex, she'd be downstairs wearing a T-shirt that says *Check the Attic*." John was roaring at this point, and I realized that the crazier I sounded, the more he enjoyed himself. At one point, Seinfeld came up in conversation, and I said, "Remember when you went on Leno? It was cruel seating you next to Seinfeld. He looked pretty good, then *you* sat down next to him and suddenly his hair looked fried and bald and his eyes were like an inch apart!" We cracked up, and it was then I realized that Carolyn was right when she kept insisting that John just wanted to hang out and have a laugh.

John paid the bill and we left. I insisted that he take the first cab we found so I wouldn't have to worry about leaving him alone on the curb with all the bridge-and-tunnel riffraff. As his cab pulled away, I watched the silhouette of his head through the cab window and thought how normal he looked, just like everyone else. I couldn't find my own cab and walked home.

Although I had nothing to really run home to, my life felt enormously full. After a childhood as a loner, I had learned to be content with my own company and was never bored. However, each time I turned the key in my apartment door I heard my grandmother's voice: *"In order to be truly happy, you must have a living thing in your home."* I bought a large banana palm, and solved *that* problem.

About a week after our dinner at Florent, John and I were trying to come up with a cover idea for our October 1997 issue. I

looked over the editorial lineup and saw an article on famous female spies throughout history. Remembering our discussion about
Austin Powers, I suggested dressing the film's heroine, Elizabeth
Hurley, as different female spies. John agreed that it would be
a no-brainer: She was the face of Estée Lauder, and that would
please the fashion crowd, who were big advertisers, particularly
in the fall.

THE SHOOT

ELIZABETH HURLEY

We phoned Elizabeth's production company and spoke with her
longtime publicist, Karin Smith. Then we started compiling a list
of spies for Elizabeth to portray. The choices ranged from Mata
Hari to Josephine Baker. We planned to shoot several characters for inside the magazine, but we struggled to find sexy op-
tions that were cover-worthy for our "Spy Issue." We eventually
settled on a generic *Austin Powers*–style Elizabeth in a Versace
dress and boots, holding a gun.

Prior to meeting Elizabeth I expected the worst—a glamorous
and pretentious English snob. She arrived looking like a star, in a
lavender wool coat with a dyed lavender fur collar, but she turned
out to be more like a brunette version of Carolyn to me; she got
all the jokes, she was funny, and we were around the same age.

Elizabeth created a lighthearted atmosphere in the studio.

We were working with the photographer Michael Thompson, who always made women look beautiful and radiant, and Elizabeth insisted on the best hair and makeup: Serge Normant and Laura Mercier. Elizabeth sailed through the shots, taking breaks to smoke Silk Cut cigarettes here and there. As she stamped out each cigarette she'd sing out, "Lau-ra! Serge!" signaling she was ready for a touch-up or a costume change.

We ran into an issue on the third character, Josephine Baker. Claire Todd, the stylist, came over to me to explain that the Josephine Baker costume was basically a lot of feathers with a tiny clamshell that needed to be attached to cover up the bikini area. The problem was that Elizabeth wouldn't be able to wear anything under it.

Claire walked over to Elizabeth, who was half dressed, and before she could explain the predicament, Elizabeth said, "Come on, love, just snap it on!" A few minutes later I heard Elizabeth getting into the jazz age–era mood by humming "Le Jazz Hot" from the film *Victor Victoria*. It reminded me of all the kids in the music-theater department at Carnegie Mellon.

When the magazine came out, Elizabeth sent John a thank-you note. As soon as he read it, he came out of his office, rolling his eyes as he read me the last line, "'And please give my regards to the adorable Matt Berman.' Oh, Jesus," John sighed. "What the hell happened down at *that* shoot?" I gave John a half smile and shrugged my shoulders. She was a charmer.

A couple of months later a group from *George* attended a benefit at the Armory on Lexington Avenue, and I spotted Elizabeth waiting near the restrooms. RoseMarie pleaded with me, "Say hi, Matt. You liked her so much." "Oh, come on," I replied, "she won't remember me. I'll look like a stalker. Let's just go." But Rose wouldn't stop nudging me, so I walked over and parked myself right in front of her. "Elizabeth . . ." I started. She stared at me, slightly blank for an instant, then in recognition exclaimed, "Adorable Matt!" She remembered me *and* saved my ass from embarrassment in front of my coworkers, who I was trying to impress. We chatted amiably until Hugh Grant came out of the men's room and Elizabeth introduced him to the group. I had mileage for a month at the office over this episode. I guess I was testing Elizabeth to see if she was as cool as she'd been on set.

Rose and I always analyzed the behavior of the stars we met. Usually, it was the ones we least expected to be down to earth who turned out to be *real* people: Robert De Niro, Howard Stern, and Pamela Anderson, for example. Spending eight hours with these people through hair and makeup, lunch, shooting, and chitchat gave me a sense of what they were really like. I knew that I got special attention from stars for being John's representative at a shoot, but I was developing my own persona. I had plenty of opportunity to use my own humor and charm to get noticed apart from being John's creative director, and that instilled me with the confidence John had always had in me even when I'd lacked it myself.

Publicists were often terrified of their star bosses and scrambled to keep them happy. Once the publicist of a major star cornered me near the end of a photo shoot in a panic. "He and his wife think I've screwed up this whole day," she confided. I tried to soothe her but as I turned away she grabbed my wrist. "When we get into the elevator later, I want you to say out loud that I did a great job." I thought she was a lunatic. Later as the publicist, the star and his wife, and I rode down in the elevator I felt a jab in my side. I looked and saw the publicist pleading with her eyes as she mouthed, "Do it, do it," like a psycho. She looked so scared that I took pity on her. "Well, it was a long day for all of us, but you did a really good job," I said. Her terror transformed into satisfied smugness as she chimed back, "Thank you, Matt!" I used to leave these awkward star situations appreciating how naturally everyone could behave around John.

John looked like a star, but he never behaved like one. He talked to movie stars the same way he talked to anyone else. No one impressed him simply because they were famous. Why would they? He himself was famous before he even knew his own name, so he didn't put much stock in celebrity alone. Still, I never could see a difference in his attitude or demeanor; no matter who John was dealing with, he always behaved exactly the same way with everyone he met.

Rose was on the subway with John once, and a young black guy asked John, "Why don't you have any black people on the cover of *George*?" (There seemed to be an unofficial rule that black covers could run in months when the advertising and the magazines were slimmer, usually January or July.) We laughed as Rose told me how she was thinking, *Please don't say it, please don't say it,* and then cringed as John answered, "Well, magazine publishers are always telling me that black covers don't sell."

Many people have shared their recollections of John with me over the years, and they all seem to have similar stories about his authenticity. A friend of mine named Matt used to work as a waiter at a restaurant called Bodega near John's apartment in Tribeca. John would often stop in, take a seat at the bar to watch a game, and shoot the shit with Matt. One Sunday morning, John walked in with Carolyn through a flurry of flashbulbs and took a seat in a far corner of the restaurant, away from the front windows and the lurking paparazzi. John said to Matt, "We hate to ask you, but would you mind grabbing a couple of newspapers for us?" The newspapers were kept by the windows, and John didn't want to give the photographers any more pictures. Pouring some coffee, Matt said, "Wow, I can't imagine what that is like. How do you *deal* with that?" John, taking a slurp of coffee, said, "Why don't you walk home with us and see for yourself."

John had this amazing down-to-earth way about him that made everyone feel automatically at ease around him, including me . . . which is why I hoped he was planning to come to the Barbara Walters shoot, which I had a feeling was going to be tough.

THE SHOOT

BARBARA WALTERS

None of the *George* photographers were excited to shoot our next cover, Barbara Walters. We'd booked the best in the business to shoot Robert De Niro after making one phone call. Claudia Schiffer nude wasn't a tough one to dole out either. I could have lowered *George*'s standards and hired a less celebrated photographer, but John and our readers were used to seeing covers shot by stars of the fashion world. I racked my brain trying to think who I knew well enough to ask for the favor of shooting *this* one. It finally came to me: Wayne Maser—he never let me down.

"Absolutely not!" Cindi Berger, Barbara Walters's publicist, barked. "I've worked with Wayne Maser before. He's a *nightmare,* and Barbara will *hate* him."

I knew that Wayne had a reputation. He'd smashed a few cameras in his day. He'd made models cry. Wayne himself told me how he'd infuriated Al Pacino at one of his photo shoots because he'd addressed him as "Buhbie." After some prying, I found out that Cindi's problem with Wayne stemmed from the time he'd photographed one of her clients, Johnny Depp, for *Interview.* Wayne had promised to touch out the tattoo on Depp's arm, which read "Winona Forever," but he'd "forgotten" to do so. We tried a tactic on Cindi that we had learned from John. "Well, we've called everybody; the only photographer available is Wayne Maser."

"Matt, I'm not putting Barbara and Wayne Maser in the same room!" she insisted.

My voice swelled with disappointment. "Maybe this cover's just not in the stars this month."

We were on for the following Wednesday.

"You're going to ruin my career," Wayne whined. "You only assign me the covers that no one else wants." It was 9:00 a.m., and we were sitting in the glass-walled coffee bar of Pier 59 Studios on the banks of the Hudson River. Wayne was wearing what he always wore—a tight, hand-tailored pinstriped suit, custom-made in London. The way he slumped at the counter, with one hand in his wild, longish gray hair and the other cradling his coffee cup, made him look thirty years old at first glance. But sunlight streaming in the window revealed he was closer to fifty. His good looks were weathered from years of hard work, hard play, and chasing or breaking up with a stream of glamorous girlfriends. Wayne took a sip of coffee. "This is the worst cappuccino I've ever had." Smiling, he looked directly at the *only* person behind the counter and said, "Who the hell made this?" His constant teasing always made me laugh.

"Keep your head down!" Wayne mumbled in a "top secret" voice. I looked across the room and saw that Barbara Walters had arrived an hour early, along with Cindi and her entourage. She looked imposing in her long coat and high heels, the fluff of hair on top of her head like cotton candy. Wayne looked at me in complete disappointment. "Why do I get all the old broads to shoot?" he pouted, then added, "and it's my birthday today!"

We saw Barbara point a finger toward the studio and march off in that direction. Our heads were practically *on* the coffee bar as she clicked by. "Wayne, shouldn't we go say hello?" I said, knowing she was going to be met by his assistants, who wouldn't know what the hell to do with her. Wayne lit a cigarette and said, "Drink your coffee, she'll wait."

In the studio I saw Barbara standing in the middle of the room, amidst the lights and electrical cables, looking around skeptically. I rolled my eyes at Wayne and strutted across the room to introduce myself.

"Hi, Ms. Walters, I'm Matt, from *George*."

"Matt from 'Doitch'?" she asked, not understanding me.

"No, Matt, from *George* magazine," I enunciated, putting my hand out. Sensing her disappointment, I added, "John's going to come down a bit later to say hello to you."

"John who?" she asked.

Cindi gave me a cool hello, and the three of us walked over to where Wayne was fiddling with his camera. I put my hand on Wayne's shoulder. "Ms. Walters, this is Wayne Maser, the photographer." Barbara stared at Wayne like a cartoon character that'd been struck by Cupid's arrow. "What a *fabulous*-looking man you are. How do you stay so trim?" As they chatted about Wayne's workout routine, I called the office.

"Rose? It's Matt."

She asked, "Is it crazy down there? Does she hate Wayne?"

"You're *not* going to believe it," I said. "It's *Love Story* down here."

I filled Rose in while Barbara browsed through the dozens of outfit choices we'd brought for her. Then I went over to Wayne and said, "Let's go over there and see what she likes."

"Stay outta there! We'll look like a couple of old queens," Wayne said, lighting another cigarette.

Barbara slammed through each hanger on the rack. A long red Bill Blass gown, an Yves Saint Laurent gown, some Jil Sander suits, ten Ralph Lauren dresses, Prada, Versace, Hermès, and fifty more pieces from Bergdorf's. "None of these are going to do. I've brought some of my own things." She unzipped a huge garment bag and pulled out a few of those knee-length, bell-shaped dresses that uptown ladies wear to charity events. She chose one and went behind a screen to change. She spun out from behind the screen like a toy top, the top half white and the bottom half yellow. If she would only wear the long red Bill Blass gown, she would *at least* look elegant. "Wayne, she *loves* you!" I pleaded, "Ask her to wear it." Moments later, our Lady in Red stepped onto the set, faithfully following her Svengali's wishes.

The cover line John wanted to use was *What Makes Barbara Walters Cry?* Barbara wedged herself between stacks of televisions glowing with images of the celebrities she'd brought to tears over the years. Wayne started snapping. Looking at the Polaroids, we could see something wasn't working. The picture would be a lot funnier if she'd laugh to offset the teary stars displayed on the televisions around her. Then, as if she'd read my mind, Barbara said, "Norman Parkinson once took a fabulous picture of me with my head thrown back, laughing madly." "Let's try it!" I shouted eagerly from the wings. She lifted her arms high above her head and roared with wicked laughter in the flame-red dress. Wayne turned to me, shrugged his shoulders, and said, "She looks like my aunt Lil!"

John entered with a smile on his face—RoseMarie had obviously filled him in on the love fest. Wayne finished shooting, and everybody gathered around John. Barbara came over to say hello.

"You have wonderful color. Did you go somewhere warm?" Barbara asked him.

"Yeah, I just interviewed the Dalai Lama in Tibet, then I took a couple of days and went kayaking with a friend," John answered as frankly as he always did.

"Wonderful," Barbara said, mesmerized by John.

John and I walked over to the buffet table. John grabbed a bunch of grapes, munching them in handfuls. Barbara had changed into a terry-cloth bathrobe and was writing at a small table by the window, telephone receiver to her ear. "John, where was it *exactly* you went kayaking?" she asked. John looked over at me in disbelief. She was obviously talking to the writers of her television show, *The View.* Hesitantly he answered, "Tibet." "What was the name of the river?" she impatiently asked. John, horrified, answered, "The Yangtze." John quickly said good-bye and bolted before she turned the encounter into a full-fledged interview. John was used to an off-the-cuff conversation becoming "news."

Barbara chose another outfit and started to pose again. At this point we had the shot we wanted, so it didn't really matter. Wayne was shooting film, and I could tell Barbara was feeling pretty good, sexy. Somehow, she found out that it was Wayne's birthday. In her famous Barbara Walters way, she exclaimed, "After the shoot we should all celebrate at some wonderful outdoor Mexican restaurant and *drink margaritas!*"

A few days later, I went down to Wayne's to edit the film. Wayne was complaining about his landlord, who had just jacked up the rent on his picturesque town house apartment facing Gramercy Park. We went through the contact sheets and I settled on an image. "Well, you had your chance to be Wayne Walters."

"How do you know I haven't called her?" Wayne said as he handed me two photos that he liked better than mine, then added, "Yeah, maybe you're right. I'd be loaded now!"

The red dress had been a good idea. Once it was on the newsstands, Barbara sent John a note: "I love my cover, I love Wayne Maser, and I love *George!*"

As hard as we all worked at *George,* John managed to offset the long hours by creating a fun-loving vibe around the office. Always sincere, he had a tendency to say whatever happened to be on his mind. His sincerity often led to teasing—and no one in the office was safe. His teasing was harsh, but because he made the effort to get to know the staffers personally, the harshness somehow felt like intimacy. No article of clothing went unnoticed by John. There were outfits you'd only be able to wear to the office once. Ned Martel, in his Southern gentleman, seersucker suit, became Colonel Sanders. Biz Mitchell, in a pink skirt, edged on the bottom with black fringe that swung as she walked, was Gypsy Rose Lee. Rose, in her new pair of Manolo Blahniks, was Pamela Anderson Lee. Rich Blow, in his knitted vests, Mister Rogers, and anyone wearing the latest Adidas or Nikes was called Homey.

There was no escape from John's critiques. When John interviewed Fidel Castro in Cuba, a British senior editor named Inigo accompanied him. On their return, John made the rounds at the office, entertaining the editors with the details of his conversation with his father's onetime nemesis. When he got to my office, knowing the interview wouldn't interest me much, he highlighted the part of the trip he knew would make me laugh. "So, Maestro, the day after, we all went to the beach, and Inigo wore a big straw hat and had his boxers turned around so you couldn't see his who-zee." I loved that he noticed the subtlest details.

The more obvious targets were like shooting fish in a barrel for John. Strolling past Rose's desk once on a humid day in August, John said to me, "Hey, Matt, is it Halloween today?" He waited a beat before adding, "Then why does Rosie have that fright wig on?" I laughed. I guess she hadn't blow-dried her hair that sticky New York summer morning and it had sprung back into her natural curls. Like a little sister being teased by her brothers, Rose said, "Shut up, Matt, don't laugh at him!" and socked John hard on his arm. I had to laugh, because I knew how hard *she'd* be laughing when I was his target.

I once found John and Rose sitting in front of his computer after working on an interview for hours. He pointed out that a word was misspelled and Rose said, "I know, I know, I'm not stupid!" John looked over at her with false sincerity and said, "Oh, Rosie, I'd *never* call you stupid." He stroked her head tenderly and said, "That would be like calling a short person 'short'!" The closer John felt to someone, the harsher and more personal his ribbing became—that was just how he expressed intimacy. John was wild about Rose—when she wasn't there, he wandered around the office, lost—which meant he tortured her the most.

Anticipating John's heckling, I'd make it easy for him and give him ammunition with which to torture me. I was convinced I was rapidly losing my hair, and no one found my panic funnier than John did. It seemed as if his hair was thickening at the same pace that mine was thinning. I told him, "It's like you and I are two beaches right next to each other. My beach is eroding and your beach is gaining all the sand!" One afternoon, John was in his office having his hair cut by one of Carolyn's friends when I heard him shout, "Where's Matt Berman, where's Matt Berman?" His tone prepared me for some major teasing. He was holding a brown Food Emporium bag filled with his freshly cut hair. I shook my head in mock disappointment. "How could you be so cruel? That's not funny," I said. Smiling, John replied, "Don't worry, I can give you more next time."

It wasn't often, but I savored the moments when I had the opportunity for revenge. John fractured his leg on one of his adventure weekends and arrived at work on crutches. He even had a wheelchair for getting around the office quickly. The teasing possibilities were endless, and I was in heaven. He wheeled down the hall in his pitiful wheelchair and I said, "Look at *poor* Tiny Tim. 'God bless us, every one.'" John looked up at me with a hateful look on his face and said, "Shut up and wheel me down to Eleanor's office!" I pushed him slowly down the hall, as if I'd been visiting Grandpa in the nursing home. I looked down at him with nostalgic sentimentality. "John, did you ever think it would come to this?"

We had our moments of conflict too. I remember John coming into the art room once, holding a page layout in his hands, and saying, "Matt, I was looking at this layout. Is there a way to make it more interesting? Another picture, or blast the title up or something?" My staff had worked so hard to get everything done on time, and I thought it looked great. Although John was perfectly polite as usual, I yelled, "Why don't you find a more interesting story? It isn't the layout!" I felt like a frustrated wife throwing pots and pans onto the floor, yelling, "You don't like the dinner? Cook it yourself!" Realizing that I had overreacted, I tried a quick save and said, "You know, John, it's not like I take this stuff personally." John shook his head from side to side sarcastically, announcing, "No, not *you*. You never take *anything* personally."

Of course, everything *was* personal because working with John had taken over so much of my personal life. Going to the magazine every day had become so natural that the other parts of my life felt one-dimensional. One day I lounged on the sofa in my office and vented to RoseMarie about the editorial lineup leaving no room for photographs. We moved on to critiquing the production lady's latest crazy outfit and bitching about the color printer that only printed yellow. Then on to my favorite rant: how great it must be to *be* John.

We joked a lot, but we could tell when John meant business by the tone of his voice. "We have to do something nice for Donatella Versace; she's been very supportive of the magazine." I started firing off ways to include Versace's clothing within the pages of *George*. "We can do a profile on young congressmen and dress them in Versace suits. We can cosponsor a photojournalism exhibit of war photos and have a cool opening party with lots of celebrities." John squinted and stretched his back, not yet sold on my ideas. "Think about it," he said. "That's why I have a creative director."

His comment was enough to snap me off the couch and into action. I tried to come up with something other than a celebrity wearing the Versace clothes on the cover. After all, we weren't running an ad agency. We had always avoided this whole issue by dressing our cover subjects in period costumes. That way, we never needed to pander to advertisers' demands. Eventually, I hit on an idea that John liked.

I suggested re-creating the famous painting *The Spirit of '76* by Archibald Willard, depicting three soldiers of the American Revolutionary War, two with a drum and one blowing a fife. I made Xeroxes of the painting and faxed them to a stylist, a set designer, and the Versace people in Milan. I told everyone to look at the image and think of transforming it into a rock-and-roll version of the painting. In no time the office was overrun with garment bags from Versace, filled with silver evening gowns, skin-tight boots, sequined bell-bottoms, tube tops, wildly patterned bras, and boxes of high heels. The stylist examined the clothes and went out and found Revolutionary War coats, three-cornered hats, and the like to complement the clothing. Gibson Guitars sent over a red, white, and blue electric guitar shaped like a map of the United States. The set designer rigged up a surreal haunted landscape, with twisting branches, rocks, leaves, and a post-nuclear sky replete with ominous purple clouds.

I called Satoshi Saïkusa, the Japanese fashion photographer who lived in Paris. He had no clue what *The Spirit of '76* was.

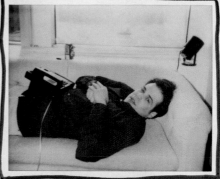

Me in my office, 1997.

My "big sister" at Hachette, Marian McEvoy.

Stephanie Mikesell, Michelle Tessler, Jennifer Heller, and Meghan Hurley covered my door in Hershey's Kisses that spelled "Matt" for my birthday.

RoseMarie Terenzio and me, 1997.

John sitting next to his gag Christmas present to the art department—a bubbling, neon plastic palm tree.

Aunt Jane Hsiang, a grown-up buddy at Hachette. The comment on the tape refers to when we flew to Los Angeles and laughed about what an awful stewardess Jane would make.

George!

Do you like Mice Lenny?

Lenny: Yeah George I like them. They're soft. Pinch their little heads.

COPIES & ENLARGEMENTS CALL 800-421-1030

I photographed everyone in the hat from Harrison Ford's cover shoot. Opposite: Araminta, our receptionist (top left), Michelle Tessler (top right), Jean-Louis Ginibre (middle left), RoseMarie Terenzio (middle right), Biz Mitchell (bottom right), Carl Robbins (bottom left). This page: John and me (top); Harrison Ford as Abraham Lincoln on the cover of George, *August 1997 (bottom). John thought I looked like a moron in my photo and put a Post-it on it with this quote from* Of Mice and Men.

*White House Correspondents' Dinner invitation—
I was seated with a typical* George *mix of people:
Larry Flint, Sean Penn, and Claire Danes (right).*

TICKET   TABLE NO. **75**

84th Annual Dinner
of the
White House Correspondents' Association

The Washington Hilton
International Ballroom
Saturday, April 25, 1998

BLACK TIE

Reception   Dinner
6:00 p.m. — Terrace   7:30 p.m. — International Ballroom

Please present this ticket to enter the Reception and Ballroom.

*Country music legend Garth
Brooks and me behind the scenes
at his cover shoot.*

*Jenny McCarthy seeking
revenge for the tongue paint job.*

Pamela Anderson and me.

*Our version of "The
Spirit of '76" that
John called "Kabuki
Spirit of '76."*

*Ben Stiller playing John for our
August 1999 issue, the last issue
John edited before he died.*

J.F.K. Jr. —

Thank You for making *my* life a living **HELL !**

maybe I can return the favor some day. from a public court of law!

Hello

why, ~~John Kennedy~~, why didn't you write back?

John received strange mail—these postcards and dozens like them—at the office every day. John dubbed this nut job "Matt's Psycho," and delivered her notes to me regularly.

One of my favorite cover stars (two times), Elizabeth Hurley, who dove into each concept wholeheartedly.

To: MATT BERMAN
Company/Dept: GEORGE
Fax number:
This message is from: ELIZABETH HURLEY
Number of pages (including cover sheet): 1

Adorable One,

Much better!

See you friday avec le sexy Texan

Love Elizabeth x x x

If transmission is incomplete, please call:

The 30th birthday card I drew for Carolyn.

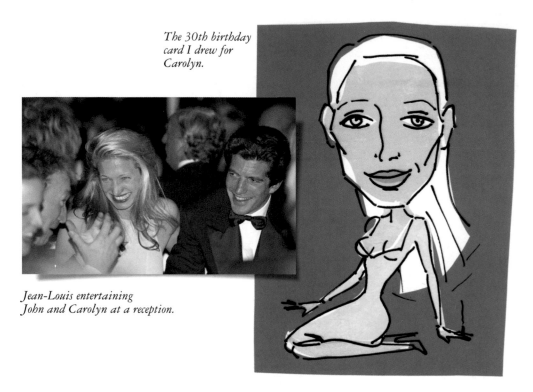

Jean-Louis entertaining John and Carolyn at a reception.

John's marriage announcement to the staff.

George

John Kennedy
Co-Founder
Editor-In-Chief

September 23, 1996

To: All the Gentlewomen and Gentlemen of *George*
From: John
Re: Breaking News

I just wanted to let you all know that while you were all toiling away, I went and got myself married. I had to be a bit sneaky for reasons that by now I imagine are obvious.

I wanted you all to enjoy these small tokens of gratitude and fellowship. You folks all do amazing work and it's an honor to have you as colleagues. This magazine has turned the corner and it ain't because fauntleroy does Oprah.

Thank you and good cheer to all.

<u>P.S.</u>   Does this mean you'll all call me <u>Mr.</u> from now on?

A Vanity Fair cartoon by Barry Blitt featuring *George covers.*

My boss, Jean-Louis Ginibre and his wife, Barbara Cady, and me (above).

My mentor, Régis Pagniez.

My file cabinet's contents: cover research—some ideas realized, some not.

George

1633 Broadway, N...
George Publishing Company,

Bruce Willis waving the American flag for an editorial shoot to appear on the interior of the magazine (top). We ended up using photos from this shoot for the cover of the memorial issue of George published in John's honor (bottom).

George

NOT JUST
POLITICS
USUAL

JOHN KENNEDY
A TRIBUTE

10 OCTOBER
1999 G
USA $4.95
CANADA $5.95
UK £2.95
Display until
November 30, 1999

03163

0 27164 8 5

"What is this painting? Famous where? I've never heard of it." Nevertheless, he agreed to the shoot because *everyone* wanted to shoot a *George* cover.

I booked three of the newest, most sought-after models of the moment: Elsa Benitez, Maggie Rizer, and the real coup, Karen Elson, who was doing every top fashion magazine cover in Europe and New York at the time. Proud that my team nailed the cover concept and bookings in less than a week's time, I marched into John's office convinced he'd be pleased. John sifted through the photos, probably hoping to see snaps of the familiar, voluptuous, tanned, longhaired goddesses he knew from the pages of the *Sports Illustrated* Swimsuit Edition—goddesses he'd dated, perhaps. Instead he stared down at skinny, pale-faced girls with dark circles under their eyes, looking like they'd just been told that their mothers were on a bus that had gone over a cliff. He looked up at me with a confused and horrified look on his face and said, "You got a Magic Marker or a pen?" I handed him a big fat Sharpie. He lined the pictures up on his desk very neatly and wrote in capital letters across all three, "YOU TOO CAN BE A MODEL, DIAL 1-800-BE-A-MODEL!" I didn't care what John thought; these were the models the fashion world was excited about. If John had done the casting, we would have ended up with a bunch of cheap pole dancers on the cover.

THE SHOOT

THE SPIRIT OF '76

The morning of the shoot, the girls arrived and sat down to have their hair and makeup done. Satoshi's makeup guy asked me how I envisioned styling the models. I didn't have anything specific in mind and told him to look at the clothes and the set, and to suggest what he thought was right. He started free-associating with a thick French accent, drawing out each syllable. "I think like something like the opera, you know, like theater. Very white and pale, with pink cheeks and red lips."

I always trust the talent I hire to bring strong ideas, and I was sure John would think it was cool. I liked the idea that we were taking an obvious American reference and twisting it into something modern and unique; *George* covers depended on this. Someone dressed up as an American hero with bad hair, bad makeup, and a lousy photographer could look lame *very* quickly. Producing them with the best talent in the fashion world is what made *George* covers cool.

John always liked things a bit flashy. He once told me that his sister had figured out a formula for buying him birthday presents. After years of gift giving, she had noticed that the gifts he responded to the most were red. And if the gift was made out of a shiny material, that was even better. Knowing his preference for red and shiny things, I was convinced he would love the drama of the cover.

The girls, dressed in their costumes, took their positions on the set, portraying a rock-and-roll version of the three "spirits." The lighting was set and we were ready for the final touches: a giant fan and a smoke machine that pumped out a rock concert haze. On the count of three, the girls lunged forward for each exposure of the camera and played their assigned instruments. The sound of Elsa's drum roused me like an eight-year-old watching a parade. The theatricality of the moment, the leaves whirling, and the models so intent and convincing made me wish that John was there to see it. It would have sold the cover to him for sure.

A few days later, the film arrived at the office. I opened the package and shut myself in my office, wondering how to approach John. The makeup looked more dramatic on film than it had looked in the studio, and the girls' faces were chalky white, ghoulish. I picked a shot with a lot of cleavage on view, threw a shiny red logo across it, and knocked on his office door, smiling from ear to ear. "I've got the cover for you to see." John twirled around from his worktable, grabbed the mock-up from my hands, and looked at me calmly after a glance at the cover. Like a schoolteacher, he said, "Matt, we wanted to redo *The Spirit of '76*"—his soft voice ratcheted up into a comical rage—"but did you have to do a *Kabuki Spirit of '76*?"

John made fun of the covers a lot, but he was the first to admit that he wasn't an artist and that he knew that the talent we were hiring to shoot the pictures, style the costumes, and do the makeup and hair were tops in the business. I was meticulous about making sure there were no weak links on a shoot. Kabuki 1776 or not, John kept an open mind and gave me the benefit of the doubt, and we sent it to the printer.

The covers might have had a lot of style, but the *George* offices didn't. There were a few visual touches, including a wall-sized *George* logo that John had made for one of the halls. Another wall was plastered with huge framed covers. But mostly, the office was drab. The editors had piles of papers everywhere, videos and books that were sent for review, snapshots of family and friends pinned up, and promotional mugs and T-shirts strewn around, not to mention a few half-eaten bagels. John wasn't into furniture, design, decorating, or art. He was given the same corner office as all the executives at Hachette, complete with the same cheesy furniture: a hideous round table like a giant hockey puck made out of light-colored wood sitting on a chrome drum. He had a view of the Hudson River on one side and a dramatic Stieglitz-style view of New York on the other.

Most of the female editors customized their offices with fancier chairs, expensive flower arrangements, and glossy magazines and books. John customized his with pairs of socks and sneakers, plastic containers of half-eaten Korean deli food, political magazines, papers, Knicks tickets, gum wrappers, and empty water bottles. Carolyn tried to cheer the place up by sending him a midcentury sofa, but when John got done throwing T-shirts and sweatpants on it, it didn't do much good.

Once you got past the mess, there were hints that you weren't in the bedroom of a typical jock. There was a black-and-white snapshot of Mick Jagger on the Kennedys' boat in Hyannis eating a giant lollypop, and another color shot of John as a boy on the shoulders of his father. There was a hideous painting of a swoosh of red paint, which John had picked out. There was a bust of George

Washington, an etching of George Washington that my mom had found while antiquing, as well as a small American flag that had gone into space with a monkey. A very large frame contained small portraits of the presidents from George Washington to John F. Kennedy, with their signatures under each one. This had belonged to John's father.

The art department was different. I liked clean surfaces at all times, the layouts updated and pinned on the wall. Film was always filed away unless we were working on it, and no personal tchotchkes or souvenirs were in evidence to clutter tabletops. I removed the fluorescent bulbs from my ceiling, threw them away, and brought in some simple modern can lights from Conran. I set a few of them on the floor, beaming upward so the place was indirectly lit. I also had the giant desk taken out. I asked the maintenance guys to build a small counter for my computer and find me a sofa and coffee table somewhere in the building. The effect was like a softly lit living room. I covered the walls with images I liked from my favorite magazines and loaded my coffee table with books and magazines.

John loved to abuse my sense of order. One day he banged on the art room door, asking his standard question: "Are you naked, can I come in?" I opened the door, and he was holding a huge cardboard box taller than he was. "Got the art department a Christmas gift." The size of the box and the tacky logo on the side—*Tropical Illusions, Miami*—spelled trouble. "Come on, let's open it!" he said enthusiastically. While John was wrestling with the box, I ran and found RoseMarie. "What the hell did he buy?" She shook a finger at me threateningly and warned me that he'd been tracking the thing down for a year.

John was on the floor like it was Christmas morning, Styrofoam and cardboard everywhere. He had the directions in one hand, and his other hand propped up a Lucite tube about seven feet long and nine inches or so in diameter. "We need six gallons of purified water, then we plug it in!" *Purified water? Plug it in?* My coworkers Carl and Michelle returned from Duane Reade with jugs of Poland Spring water. John filled the tube, snapped on a lid made of plastic palm leaves, plugged it in, and there it was, our very own, bubbling, color-changing, imitation palm tree. It was hideous. As I shook my head in disapproval, John was delighted with his destruction of the art room's serenity.

Office horseplay helped relieve the pressure and offset the grim reality that the Hachette higher-ups were scrutinizing the sales numbers. We got the results of the Kabuki 1776 cover back from sales, and it had sort of bombed. The problem, the Hachette executives told us, was that the girls' faces in the photo we preferred were too small to recognize and they had chosen to use a close-up portrait in an effort to create more impact at the newsstand. John and I disagreed, explaining that you had to see the whole photo of the three girls to understand that it was *The Spirit of '76*. As usual, when there was a slump in sales, they blamed the cover. John told me to relax, that the art direction and photos were the easiest to criticize and the easiest to change. He reminded me that promotion, good public relations, and the content of the magazine all played a part.

Outrageous costumes and modern photography had made *George* famous, but the Hachette moneymen were convinced that the covers would sell better if we had no costumes and shot everyone on a white background. Convinced they were wrong and that sales wouldn't change, John told them we'd try it.

The following month, we threw Peter Jennings's head on a cover. During the shoot, I looked at a Polaroid of Jennings's smiling head atop a white shirt and tie and felt like we'd hit rock bottom. "It looks deadly," I told the group gathered around the first Polaroid. Jennings smirked, "I don't care if you run that picture and write *BORING* across it in bold letters." He had a point; it would have been *slightly* more interesting. At least my job was easier without having to come up with actual cover concepts.

The only remnant of the old covers I insisted on continuing was hiding a small silhouette of George Washington's bust in all of the covers: on the microphone of Drew Barrymore's Marilyn, in the brooch of George Clooney's Thomas Jefferson, in some foliage around Kate Moss's Eve. It was a blatant rip-off of the hidden bunny logo on *Playboy* covers, but we always owned up to the plagiarism.

John, of course, was right, magazine sales essentially stayed the same with or without costumes on the covers, and the Hachette execs had to find other ways to boost sales. I showered John with "I told you so's" and told him we should keep trying new things.

He called his friend Meryl Poster at Miramax to see if there was an up-and-coming star to shoot. Meryl responded with an unusual name that none of us had ever heard of, Charlize Theron. She assured us that Charlize was going to be a very big deal and had movies coming out soon. I called the legendary photographer Ellen von Unwerth and described the project. "Who is she?" she asked in her German accent. "I never *heard* of her." I explained that she had some big films in the works and that she was a knock-out and used to model. "Send me her picture."

Weeks later I was in a van with Ellen, her assistants, and a stylist, heading up Columbus Avenue to pick up this unknown star. The van stopped in front of an ordinary apartment house, and Charlize jumped in. We drove to Central Park and found a bucolic setting, did Charlize's hair and makeup, and began shooting.

Charlize was full of fun and won the crew over with her charm. When I look at that cover now, it's one of my favorites, but I don't have the slightest idea what we intended when we shot it. I think we were going for a sexy Martha Washington theme. Charlize in smoky eye makeup, squeezed into a corset, wearing a three-cornered hat, with a finger in her mouth and a lipstick kiss on her boob, looked more like a Revolutionary War hooker, but a fantastic one, fit for a president.

The reality was that we got more press when the covers were more provocative. *Entertainment Tonight* and *Extra* often wanted to book me to talk about them. Most months, a camera crew would show up at the office and I would walk them through how we created the cover. Our publicist, Nancy Haberman, planned things this way, knowing I was more relaxed when I could show sketches and costumes or outtakes. When it was just a camera on my face and a reporter nodding up and down, I was uncomfortable.

After my first interview aired, John strode down the hallway at *George,* saying, "Where is Matt Berman, that *telegenic* personality?" "That bad?" I asked him. "No, but let me give you a trick. When you don't know the answer to something, look *up* toward the ceiling; it looks as if you're thinking." *Yup, that bad,* I thought. I must have looked like I was being interviewed in prison.

Making *George* each month was becoming easy for me, the celebrity schmoozing and office politics, not so much. John helped me navigate all of that, often using old-fashioned sayings that I've found useful since. He'd say, "A fish rots from the head," meaning a bad leader corrupts the whole team. Or one of my favorites: "Why does a dog lick his balls?" Answer, "Because he can—don't let him get away with it." John had a collection of simple analogies and sayings to fit all situations. They helped me understand and negotiate the landmines at *George*, and have continued to get me through challenges I've faced over the years.

8.

WHAT'S THE USE OF TALKIN'?

Early into our second year of publication, word on the street was that the honeymoon was over between the publishers and *George.* The Hachette guys thought our period costumes disguised the stars on the covers and diminished their star power; apparently the first covers were *too* avant-garde for them. But after a few more covers with boring heads on them, we felt we needed to change something and figured humor was the answer.

John had been asking me to include political cartoons in the magazine from the beginning. I had interviewed a lot of cartoon editors and met with a few well-known cartoonists, but I hadn't found the right fit. I thought we could do a photo satire like they did in *National Lampoon,* with models and actors in cartoon panels. I'd earned plenty of points with John and felt confident enough to approach him with this potentially expensive idea.

I planned a shoot that would parody the Monica Lewinsky scandal, which was dominating the news at the time. I walked into John's office holding a print of "The Loneliest Job," George Tames's famous photograph of President Kennedy looking wearily out of the south window of the Oval Office. "Hey, John, you know this picture, right?" John looked at me skeptically before saying a word. I continued, "I thought we could do a funny parody of the Lewinsky scandal with a political photo cartoon of a ravishing female president seducing a poor innocent male intern. We can hire Ellen von Unwerth to shoot a sexy model and pose her exactly like your father in this photo to open the story and title it 'That's MRS. President to YOU.'" I knew it was a touchy request, so I held on to my balls and waited for John's reaction.

"That's hilarious," he said. "Go for it."

Between scouting locations and wrangling models, sets, and props, a photo spread like this was more work than a cover shoot. Ellen suggested the New Zealand bombshell Kylie Bax to play Mrs. President. Jennifer Miller, my new photo editor, and I began to cast the rest of the characters. We found our innocent intern in a Prada model named Eric Vincent, then hired some of our old buddies from the De Niro *Casino* cover shoot—character actor buddies of De Niro who lived in Little Italy—as extras. We did a little "cruel casting" and hired a burly man to play the part of

Linda Tripp. Dolled up with a cheap wig and lipstick, he was perfect. The stylist, Andrew Richardson, dressed Kylie in tight Yves Saint Laurent outfits and outdid himself putting our butch Linda in a tacky royal blue power dress.

Watching Ellen at work, it became clear why she is a star photographer in the same league as Terry Richardson and Helmut Newton. She captures images that are chic but have a sense of humor. Once, after a fashion photographer asked Hillary Clinton to change from a navy blue turtleneck sweater into a black one, we all laughed when Hillary gave the group a deadpan look and said, "Will it really make a difference?" The fashion world in general can be a bit of a no-fun zone. I watched as Ellen scanned the set with a look of frustration and disappointment until something clicked. Then her fingers started stretching and moving, signaling her assistant to hand her a loaded camera.

We set up shop at a classic courthouse in midtown, not far from the office, and went shot to shot from my storyboard. I wish I had a sound recording of that day to laugh at again. Our hideous version of Linda Tripp pushed our poor little intern's face into her comically padded bosom, assuring him, "My dear, you can tell Auntie Linda anything. What did that mean lady do to you?" She thrust a giant flower pin clipped to her lapel, which camouflaged a microphone, toward his mouth. One of my favorite shots was Kylie as Mrs. President looking stricken surrounded by priests and nuns and wearing a YSL number open to her navel, displaying her luscious cleavage.

Senior editor Jeffrey Podolsky took out-of-context quotes from the actual trial, which we used to caption the images. The photo of Linda and the intern said, "Oh, Linda, I don't know what I'm going to do." A shot of Kylie as the sultry president with red lips and high heels, sitting in court being interrogated, was captioned, "I will instruct my attorneys to *mount* a vigorous defense." The shoot was a home run, John loved it, readers wrote in to praise it, and we got a lot of attention from the fashion advertisers, who were featured costuming all the characters.

THE SHOOT

BEN STILLER

After the success of my Mrs. President shoot, I hired Ellen again for our July humor issue. John had the idea to invite Ben Stiller to guest-edit the magazine. His editor's letter was entitled "I'm in Charge Here." Ben assigned articles to humorists like Peter Farrelly, who wrote about working on Jimmy Carter's campaign, and to his father, Jerry Stiller, who reported on the importance of Viagra in the Oval Office. I thought it would be funny if Ben, as guest editor, dressed and acted like John for the photos that accompanied his monthly column If I Were President. I ran the idea past John, and the only part that registered was that Ben Stiller was coming to the office to do a photo shoot. I wasn't sure if John understood that Ben Stiller would be playing *him*, but I forged ahead with the plan.

The morning of the shoot, stylist Wendy Schecter sent Italian suits, wingtip shoes, pale-colored shirts, and silk ties to the office, which didn't pique John's curiosity in the least. We unpacked boxes containing a kayak, surfboard, basketballs, skis, bicycle, hockey sticks, footballs, Kangol caps, and dark sunglasses. I shouted into John's office, "John, can I get into your office with the prop guys to set things up?" "Like lights and stuff?" he called back.

"And some other stuff too," I replied.

John got up from his table, dipped under a surfboard, and asked, "What's *this* for?" Sure enough, John had no clue that he was to be the butt of the joke. Meanwhile, I had already sold the idea to all of Ben Stiller's people and hired Ellen von Unwerth to photograph it. They were mere minutes from arriving. I was dead.

I took a deep breath and explained the shoot to John, showing him drawings of the scenes we'd be photographing. "He's going to walk into the building dressed like you; pin-striped suit, Kangol cap on backward, sunglasses, and carrying a bicycle wheel." John looked at me skeptically. "Matt, nobody's going to get that. You *know* me, so it's funny. People picking up the magazine aren't going to get it." I'd forgotten that John, although larger than life to most people, was just John in his own mind. Despite being photographed by the paparazzi at every turn, he had no clue that the general public had any sense of his personal style. He continued, "And then what happens, Matt?" I said, "Ben will be at your desk with a nameplate in front of him with your name crossed out and his name penciled over it. Then he'll be standing over the light table in the art room editing film."

John interrupted. "And where do all the kayaks and the volleyballs come in?"

Awkwardly trying to finesse things, I said, "Well, I thought we could pack your closet with sports stuff: bikes, skis, balls, rackets." John cut in again. "Oh, and Stiller opens the closet and is like . . ." John flailed his arms around with a moronic look on his face—"WOAHHHHHHHHH!" pretending to be avalanched by sporting goods. Relieved that he got the idea, I exhaled. "Exactly!" "Oh, I get it. You're making fun of me." "Yeah," I said, chuckling, trying to rouse a smile from John. "Matt, let me ask you something. Do you think they're over there at *Vogue* walking around wearing big sunglasses making fun of Anna Wintour?" I imagined the imperious Wintour sending someone to the guillotine. "No, but I don't think she has your sense of humor," I said.

At that moment Ellen von Unwerth came into the office. She'd caught the tail end of the conversation. "Oh, am I in trouble?" she said in her thick German accent. John stood between me and Ellen, put his arms around us, and said, "Ellen here has a prosperous career working with many different magazines. More important, she gets to leave here in a few hours." He put me in what I hoped was an affectionate headlock. "Matt, unfortunately, has only one job and has to remain here working with me!"

Luckily, John was joking, only pretending to be mad. It was easy to tell the difference, because when he was angry, a vein would pop out on his forehead and he raised his voice. The reality was that since John wasn't an artistic person, and *George* was a political magazine with no fashion editors or other creatives on staff, I had complete authority over these shoots. This has rarely happened again in my career; there are always people who want to add their two cents, take over, or even claim credit for a creative shoot. Of course, when you're in these situations, it's customary to say that everything is a *team effort* or that it's a *collaborative process,* but the best work I've done in my career, I've done on my own. Too many chefs spoil the broth, and I prefer to work toward one clear vision.

The humor issue came out with a photo I'd chosen of Ben Stiller as John on the cover, sharpening pencils in an electric pencil sharpener shaped like Bill Clinton's head. After all of

John's faux threats, he laughed out loud when he saw the opening spread of Ben holding up two *George* covers, one a head shot of Strom Thurmond, the other a sensual shot of Catherine Zeta-Jones wearing a backless halter gown. The magazine looked fun again. Although there was a lot of talk about the inside of the magazine, with its long, dense articles not matching the joyful tone of the covers, it looked fun on the newsstand. People *were* judging this book by the cover, and we were fine with that because the issue was selling.

Humor in general set the tone at *George,* and John surrounded himself with people who "got the jokes." Carolyn, Rose, John's business partner, Michael Berman, and Nancy Haberman were all quick with the one-liners. I got to know Nancy when she joined me on a trip to Los Angeles for a Chevy Chase shoot that was to be part of a series, *Rebels and Revolutionaries*, a photo essay about famous American activists. For the cover we painted Julia Roberts silver and superimposed her head onto a Susan B. Anthony coin. For the interior, we photographed John Cusack as Abbie Hoffman, Cheech Marin as Che Guevara, and Whoopi Goldberg as Rosa Parks. Chevy would play Paul Revere. At five feet tall, Nancy was a pint-sized, brunette version of Joan Rivers. We boarded the plane to L.A. and took our seats in business class.

Nancy sighed and rolled her eyes. "Matt, do you notice anything strange here?"

I looked around the cabin, examining the other passengers and flight attendants. "No, seems pretty normal." Nancy, exasperated, said, "Look at me!" The plane was charging loudly down the runway. I raised my voice and said, "You look great, Nancy, what are you talking about?" The wheels lifted off the tarmac and Nancy gave up. "Matt, my feet aren't touching the floor!" Short jokes were her specialty.

We stayed at the Four Seasons. Nancy couldn't deal with the crustiness of the Chateau Marmont, and since we were sharing a car, I coped with all the chintz and pillows at the Four Seasons. I was bummed not to stay at the Chateau, which always made me feel like I was in old Hollywood, but the beds were better at the Four Seasons, and there was a huge pool. The next day we drove to the studio to meet Chevy Chase. It was nice to have Nancy with me on the shoot so I didn't feel so alone when, as always, the people in the room realized that John Kennedy was *not* coming.

Chevy hammed it up in his three-cornered hat, holding a lantern and riding a horse. I understood why he was who he was; the picture had comic energy and it worked. After the shoot, Chevy brought over the questionnaire he had filled out for the magazine's back page. Nancy and I listened as he read his answers to John's questionnaire out loud. Nancy and I chuckled at the first few responses. Chevy got louder and more dramatic with each punch line, and we laughed harder. As Chevy continued, we were howling. In between laughs, Nancy whispered, "Matt, do you think this is funny?" I replied, "No, not at all!" This really made us laugh harder, to the delight of our star. Chevy wasn't like John, who always said, "Don't blow smoke up my ass" or "Tell me what you *really* think."

Nancy and I became fast friends, and after returning to New York, we spoke to each other often. Aside from our laughs, I think she needed me to gauge the temperature in the office, whether John was in a good mood or whether I had heard something interesting that was happening. She was an expert at extracting information. "Matt, I have a feeling John's angry about something." I answered, "No, he's not mad at you at all." "Are you sure, Matt? Because I have a feeling." "Nancy, he's *not* mad. In fact, he was just saying, 'Nancy is doing a great job.'" I had walked into her trap. "Matt, if John told you that Nancy is doing a great job, then that means that *somebody* must have said, 'Nancy is doing a *bad* job.' Who was it, Matt?"

One day I wasn't able to take Nancy's calls. She kept calling, and I kept missing her. My assistant, Stephanie, put a yellow Post-it on my computer screen each time Nancy called. By midafternoon, there was a collage of yellow Post-its on the screen, all reading, "Nancy called," "Nancy called," "Nancy called," in different colored Sharpie ink. John saw it and cracked up.

By the end of the day, not being able to get through on the phone, Nancy showed up at *George*. She walked into my office and saw the Post-its. "Great. Another way you make fun of me at this office. Matt, take those down. If John were to see those . . ." I felt a little guilty about this inside joke, but it was harmless enough because I knew that John was crazy about her. We all loved Nancy because she was like a Jewish mother watching out for us.

After that trip to Los Angeles, I circled the floors of the building, saying hello to all of my cronies. I did a double take as I passed the desk belonging to Gina, Marian McEvoy's secretary. Marian was busy watering her giant palm plants, so I stopped by to chat. "Hey, Rat, how was L.A.?" she asked. (*Rat* was short for Matt-a-Rat—as Marian explained, "Because he's a naughty, *bad* little brother. He's a *rat*!") "Marian, is Soon-Yi Previn sitting next to Gina, or am I totally crazy?" "*Yes, that is* Soon-Yi." Soon-Yi was on the cover of every tabloid that week after Mia Farrow had found naked pictures of her in Woody Allen's apartment. "Marian, what is she doing here at *Elle Decor,* of all places?" I asked. "Now, Rat, she's just a high school student, and she's friends with Gina's daughter, Lexie." Marian clapped her hands over a waste can, cleaning the soil from her palms. "Matt, you remember Lexie!" Marian lived on Planet Decor and couldn't understand why I was so surprised to see Soon-Yi outside of the tabloids and sitting right on our floor at Hachette. I walked down the hall to Peggy Russell's office, where Peggy told me, "Yes, Matt, it's a circus here."

We continued shooting the series *Rebels and Revolutionaries* in New York. I asked John if he'd come down to the studio and say hello to Whoopie Goldberg. His visits always raised the energy level at the shoots.

We were re-creating the historic event when Rosa Parks refused to move to the back of the bus. I rented a rounded 1960s bus, complete with period advertisements lining the interior walls. I had a hatmaker replicate the hat Rosa Parks wore that day. Whoopi arrived on location and seemed impressed with our preparations. Hands on her hips, she looked up at the massive old bus and said, "Wow, you guys weren't kidding."

We had a variety of vintage clothing for Whoopi to try, but she was determined to copy the old photographs exactly. She talked to each person in the room about their jobs and seduced everyone with her sincerity. We gathered around her, and she told us the real story of Rosa Parks.

"Do you know what she said to the bus driver when he asked her to move to the back of the bus?"

Several of us shouted out, "She said she wouldn't" or "She said no."

Whoopi said, "Yeah, but do you know what she *actually* said? What she said was, 'I *can't* move to the back of the bus because I'm *tired*.'" From that moment on, everyone was determined to do a perfect tribute.

Whoopi sat on a faded, vinyl seat a few rows back from the front of the bus. The battered seat was perforated with small holes, like a nurse's shoe. I positioned a few people around her to make the bus seem full. Whoopi let out a long, tired breath and drifted off into character. Her wide smile faded, her vibrant eyes dimmed, and her arms dropped listlessly into her lap. The faded grays and sad blues of the bus interior helped set the solemn mood. It began to rain.

I saw John whizzing up next to the curb on his bike. He was wearing a beret and his weird transparent Paul Smith raincoat. (I often teased him about that raincoat, and he bought me one for Christmas that year.) He got off his bike and onto the bus. John moved slowly down the aisle until he was standing right in front of Whoopi. Although Whoopi had never met John, she remained in character, her eyes looking past him.

"Excuse me, miss," John said, a stern look on his face, pointing his finger to his right. "Would you mind moving to the back of the bus?" John couldn't keep it together and began to laugh. Whoopi's face exploded into a giant smile. "Not a chance, buddy!"

Most nights after work, Rose and I would cab it straight down to Il Cantinori on Tenth Street. Since John and Carolyn were regulars there, the owner, Frank, treated me and Rose like VIPs. He always gave us a table, and if there wasn't one available, he'd have one brought up from downstairs and wedged in somewhere. At Il Cantinori, we'd hold court by the bar, because everyone would come there to smoke. We'd ham it up, fueled by martinis and red wine, saying hello to the fancy people we'd meet there, and then draw dinner out until 1:00 a.m. We'd discuss everything, from who we couldn't stand that day at the office to how, for health reasons, we should start our mornings at Il Cantinori with martinis and pasta and have the day to work it off, and then end the day with a coffee. We were sure we could lose weight this way.

Rose's dad and my grandpa Sam were both old-time Bronx guys, and we'd use all their old expressions. Their dated references made us laugh. We called JFK airport by its original name, Idlewild. We asked each other, "What the hell's a matter with you?" We ended most conversations with "What's the use of talkin'?" We laughed that her dad and my grandpa would say we were like William Powell and Myrna Loy. Even today, when Rose and I meet for a night on the town, we say, "We're Nick and Nora Charles!"

My days and nights were exciting, exhausting, and fulfilling. My social life and my work life had become one. I thought about hanging out with old friends and family, but nothing felt as good as learning about decor with Marian, listening to Aunt Jane's crazy stories over drinks, hanging out with RoseMarie, John, and Carolyn, or eating out with Jean-Louis.

Everything was fun with these people. How else would I have learned all the "Jean-Louis lingo" I picked up over the years? For example, when I told Jean-Louis that an editor was cheating on his wife, Jean-Louis said, "You mean he is parking his pink Mustang on a side street?" Another time, I told him someone at the office was a pain in the ass and that she was ugly too. Jean-Louis stopped me. "Matt, you never call a woman ugly." Pausing, he added, "You say *homely*." He warned me that in France, when you say a woman is *adorable,* it usually means she is *homely* as well. I always used to call Jean-Louis to discuss business at noon, hoping to get an invitation to lunch out of the deal. He quickly caught on and said, "Matt, I know you are calling at twelve o'clock every day so you can come to lunch with me." As soon as I'd begin talking, he'd cut me off and say, "The Palm restaurant at twelve thirty." Jean-Louis was an impeccable dresser and hated "dress down Fridays," when the staff could wear what they wanted. "These people look okay in a suit, but their casual clothes are disgusting!"

I remained extremely close to Jean-Louis over the years; calling him on Sundays, emailing him for advice, and remembering his birthday. I never took for granted that Jean-Louis had proposed only *one* choice for creative director to John. I hadn't realized that his family was aware of our closeness until he died, and his son, Jean-Noel, asked me to do the eulogy at Westwood Village Memorial Park in Los Angeles; the final resting place of Marilyn Monroe, Dean Martin, and Billy Wilder. I was heartbroken telling humorous anecdotes, knowing the people who would have laughed the hardest weren't there to hear them. I looked over at my lifeless mentor, his rigid hands wrapped in a string of rosary beads, and remembered him telling me, "You know, Matt, I lived in the best time for sex; there was no AIDS, and we had penicillin for VD." As the casket door closed, a ray of light passed over his handsome face for the last time. For me, it was the end of an era.

Our office at 1633 Broadway was a world unto itself, and it was amazing. No one made me laugh like the people there. I was so immersed in my work at *George* that seeing anyone outside of the circle felt like a chore and a distraction. I didn't have time for it, and when I did have free time, I wanted to be by myself and recharge. My brothers and cousins were frustrated with me because they couldn't reach me by phone and I seldom went back to Stamford. I put most of my friends from the past on the back burner. I was like a cat with nine lives, and this life was the best one yet. I felt that if I saw my old friends, went home to the family every weekend, and left work at five instead of going out on the town, it would diminish my life at *George* and bring me back to who I was before. I liked who I'd become and didn't want to do *anything* that would change the way things were. Unfortunately, things out of my control were about to change *everything*.

9.

SEE YOU MONDAY, MAESTRO!

FOUR O'CLOCK SATURDAY MORNING,

JULY 17, 1999

I drowsily picked up my telephone; it had been ringing and ringing, and I'd been ignoring it. It was RoseMarie. She was staying at
John's apartment because her air conditioner was broken. He had
given her his keys on Friday so she'd have a comfortable weekend
while he and Carolyn were away.

"Matt," she said quietly, "it's Rose." Her cautious tone made
me think that she had flooded the bathroom or knocked over
John's father's scrimshaw collection and needed help cleaning
up the mess. "You can't go to L.A. this morning." *Here we go,* I
thought. This was too much; I wasn't postponing a cover shoot

of Rob Lowe over some broken whale teeth at the apartment on North Moore. I started working on excuses to get out of helping her, whatever she had done. In a quavering voice, she said, "John never landed last night."

I mumbled something, then got up and raised the shade to look out the window; it was still dark out. In a careful tone, she continued, "People have been calling here all night." I was silent. "Are you there?" she asked, breaking into my stupor.

"This is going to be terrible," I said as I plopped down on the edge of my bed. I thought of all the horrible possibilities. I didn't feel emotional; I was trying to process the information.

"He probably landed somewhere on the way because of the weather," Rose said. *Of course, what a relief,* I thought. *She's right. He's asleep outside Boston somewhere, thank God. John's going to wake up at the Cambridge Holiday Inn, turn on the TV, and be really embarrassed to find out that the whole world thinks he's missing.* "Oh, shit, he's going to be so pissed!" I said, chuckling, enjoying the picture in my head. "He should've called me," Rose said, sounding a little angry.

We agreed that I'd move my 8:30 a.m. flight to 11:00 a.m. "Come down here and wait with me," Rose said, excited by the impromptu breakfast party. By the time I had washed my face and gotten dressed, the story was on television. Rose called again and instructed me to call from the pay phone on the corner of John's block to avoid having to stand and ring the buzzer in front of the growing number of reporters. As I hung up I heard her say, "And bring coffee."

That the disappearance of John, Carolyn, and her sister Lauren had already made the news snapped me out of my willful denial. I needed to talk to the person who knew me best. Although it was three hours earlier in San Francisco, I called my cousin Seth (aka Bitter Seth), who I still talked to every day; given my late nights and the time difference, I could decompress by chatting with him at the end of my day. His phone rang several times, and then I heard fumbling and a groggy "Hello?" "Hi," I started to say as Seth interrupted me with "What's wrong?" Seth knew how uber-careful I was about calling him, or anyone, at annoying times, and 1:30 a.m. wasn't exactly cocktail hour. "John's plane didn't land last night," I said in a scratchy whisper. "What?" Seth answered, sounding more concerned than annoyed.

My voice became fainter as I said the words, "I think they're dead." I knew they were coming out of my mouth, but it was as if I was hearing someone else say them. I heard the snap of a cigarette lighter through the receiver, then a long exhale of smoke. "Wait a minute, tell me everything." As I retraced the evening from 5:00 p.m. at the office until now, I became stiff with fear. This *was* really happening.

I clicked into automatic mode. I took the elevator down to the lobby of my building. "Matthew," I heard Juan-Carlos the doorman say in his Spanish accent, "what's up with your boss?"

"Don't worry," I assured him in an attempt to assure myself as I walked out into the thick July heat. "He'll turn up."

I stopped at Au Bon Pain and picked up six coffees, then cabbed it over to 20 North Moore to join Rose, John's buddy, Pat, and Carolyn's friends, Jessica, Narciso, and Danny, who were all gathered there. As my cab pulled up to the curb, it was clear that Rose's instincts had proven right; there were fifteen reporters there. They were milling around the street and the steps in front of the building.

A reporter was using the pay phone across the street. I waited behind her and listened to her end of the conversation. "Yeah, I've been down here for two hours," she said, snapping her gum. "Nobody's up there, coming in or going out."

I went upstairs and said hi to everyone. The mood was solemn and serious. Narciso was on the couch, huddled in a beige cashmere blanket; Pat was in the den on another sofa with Rose. Danny and Jessica were at the dining room table, smoking. Rose worked the telephone nonstop, fielding calls through tears. Time moved so slowly. After hours of waiting, smoking, and nervously snacking and pacing, the place began to get messy. Jessica played mamma, cleaning up and putting things in their places. "You can empty an ashtray, Matt Berman," she said, nudging me to help out. She was right; I was useless and felt like I shouldn't have been there. What if John's family arrived? What were we all doing there? Somehow the others felt okay being in the apartment, but I felt out of place.

I canceled my 11:00 a.m. flight, and waited. I canceled the 1:00 p.m. flight, and waited. The situation grew more and more grim. I called Rob Lowe's people and told them that the photographer would be handling the shoot himself and that no one from *George* would be coming.

The news coverage finally confirmed our worst fears: John, Carolyn, and Lauren were officially *lost* and probably dead. I couldn't stand the grim vigil in John's apartment any longer. I decided to go up to the office. I found a cab and sat in the backseat in a daze as we barreled up Eighth Avenue. I looked out the cab windows at people bicycling, laughing in restaurants, and kissing each other good-bye. They were having normal, happy Saturday mornings. It seemed unfair that when something terrible was happening for one person, there was something wonderful happening for someone else. I thought back to the moment I was being attacked by raccoons in 1964; were Michael Caine and Julie Christie driving a Jaguar through the streets of Swinging '60s London? Did someone walk out of a Beatles concert in Las Vegas at that moment? Did someone win the lottery that day? How could these people be having a nice brunch when John was at the bottom of the sea? Fuck them!

The cab turned on West Fiftieth Street on our way to 1633 Broadway, and we passed Blockheads Mexican restaurant. John had eaten lunch there just the day before. *Perfect,* I said to myself, *John's last meal was at Blockheads.* Chefs and restaurateurs wooed him with special dishes his whole life, and the last meal he ate was a burrito, and not even the best one. I wondered about all of John's unexpected "lasts." He woke up Friday morning and got out of his bed, that was the last time. I saw him drink an iced tea on Friday, which was probably his last one. He locked up his bike outside of the building, probably for the last time.

The cab dropped me at the side door of the building, and I walked into the cavernous black marble lobby and froze. It was sinking in that *Carolyn* was dead too. That was harder to come to grips with than the fact that John was dead. Maybe it was because Carolyn was one of us, a mortal. John came from an extraordinary background, was treated like a prince his entire life, and had so many gifts and advantages. The Icarus flying too close to the sun comparison is almost too easy. Carolyn grew up in White Plains, New York, twenty minutes from Stamford. She told me that her father was in the building trades, a regular working dad like mine. She was like me, and she was dead? It seemed impossible. My mind toggled back and forth between the two of them until my head hurt.

Strangely, my first real response was anger. *You stupid asshole! Having everything wasn't enough; you had to fly airplanes too? What a spoiled brat!* Maybe he did have too much. I guess nothing was *enough*—nothing was high enough, great enough, deep enough, big enough, maybe John didn't feel like *he* was enough. His bar exam score wasn't high enough or he wasn't enough like his father.

I started to feel sorry for John, always being judged and scrutinized, and my anger turned to pity for him—and for myself for losing him.

I felt dizzy as I stepped into the elevator, pressed 41, and felt the car rise. I heard the familiar chime, and the door opened. The lobby of the floor was dark, and there was no "Good morning, Matt" from smiling Araminta, our receptionist. I beeped my code into the security pad. The door clicked, and I walked down the hallway with the *George* logo painted in two shades of orange that John and I had obsessed over. Having grown up in the '70s, we both liked orange.

I walked into John's office. The door was unlocked, and for the millionth time I thought, *I can't believe the maids don't lock this door, with those priceless mementos that belonged to John's dad.* The office, usually buzzing with activity and laughter, was a silent shrine. The air-conditioning was off for the weekend, and the room was stifling. Sneakers and stinky socks cluttered the floor, piles of manuscripts lay on the table, a plastic fork and a container from a salad bar were still damp with dressing. Most upsetting was a yellow Post-it stuck to John's phone receiver, written in red Sharpie in Rose's familiar handwriting, "Lauren downstairs in 5." I felt queasy and walked out of the room.

Down the hall, most of the staff was showing up like it was a Monday morning. The normally cool, flippant New Yorkers were stunned, unshaven, disheveled, hugging each other, sobbing, sprawled out on the floor looking at the TV news in horror. I've never been a good shoulder to cry on, so I went into my office.

I sat on my sofa and looked at the mess left over from a frantic week of work. I remembered the night before, when John was on his way out and breezed past my office, saying, "See you Monday, Maestro!" I saw only his back as I leaned out into the hall to yell good-bye. I looked for hidden meaning. *See you Monday, Maestro!* That was it? We went from "Hi, I'm John" to "See you Monday, Maestro."

I stared out my window at the Hudson River. *How could things turn so quickly?* In one minute, John was *nothing*. Just as *nothing* had turned into *everything* when I met him, *everything* turned into *nothing* when he died. So many things turned out to be the opposite of what they initially seemed. The first cover of *George* was actually a woman; the Prince and the Vampire (me) were very much alike; John's icy wife turned out to be warm and funny. The job I wasn't sure I could handle helped me come into my own. When their plane crashed into the sea, pure water turned into a brick wall.

What would happen now? Would we finish the issue we were working on? Would Hachette close the magazine? Who would want to read JFK Jr.'s magazine without JFK Jr. running the show? I knew I wouldn't.

I had thought I would work for John forever, to the point

where I'd felt a little trapped. My dreams of working in Europe, or art directing a glossy fashion magazine, or making movies had been sacrificed because of the amazing situation I'd fallen into with John and *George*. We would joke about how I could make myself useful if he became president. "What would I do in Washington?" I'd ask him. He'd laugh as I assigned myself projects like redesigning all the highway signs, or redesigning the dollar. John never seemed serious about running for president, but I admired him so much that I always thought it could happen.

I walked down the hall away from the others and sat down in the empty conference room, with its long, cheesy, varnished table. The room was dark and silent. I always hated going in there and having to listen to the editors present their story ideas. I never knew who they were talking about and just waited for them to fill out a photo sheet, which worked like Cliffs Notes for me. Photo sheets listed the subject's name, why they were relevant, whether they agreed to be photographed, or if we needed photo research or a drawing. One morning I slid into a chair next to John at that same table after a bender at Il Cantinori with Rose. I was trying to look as alert as possible. John said good morning to everyone and immediately turned the meeting over to me to explain the upcoming photography stories to the advertising department. Thinking that I had pulled myself together pretty well after a rough night, I proceeded to show boards of what the art department was working on. As I wound down, I felt John tugging on my sleeve. Smiling, he leaned over closely and whispered, "What the hell happened to you last night? Jesus, your eyes are like two slits!" I guess I should have gotten up earlier.

I left the conference room, walked down the hall, went back into my office, and shut the door. Stuck to my computer screen were two Post-it notes of cartoon faces John had doodled that made me laugh. They were of ugly men's heads, like dumb boxers. I studied them for some sort of foreshadowing but concluded that they were just ugly and John wasn't the best artist.

I found a sketch on my desk of Princess Diana in a George Washington hat, which I had given John to use to convince her to do a cover. I pounced on John when he got back from meeting her for tea at the Four Seasons. "What was she like? What happened?" He set the sketch on my desk and said, "Well, she said *no,* but she had a great pair of legs!" When Diana died, Carolyn told John that he should call the two orphaned princes, but John thought that was weird because he had never met them. I guess he would've known best on that one.

There was a contact sheet of pictures of John we had shot for an interview. Jean-Louis was right: He wasn't perfect. "He has very short teeth," Jean-Louis always reminded me. I found a photocopy of a poster of the blonde actress Carroll Baker in the film *Baby Doll*—a grown woman lying in a crib, sucking her thumb.

John had us fax it to Carolyn at home, a joke making fun of her for not working and being a lady of leisure after hustling fashion jobs for a decade. I sifted further to find a memo John sent to the staff after one of our covers knocked it out of the park with sales. "Soon Matt Berman will be able to sit bare bottomed on the Xerox machine, put it on the cover, and we'll be assured of a sellout." The staff tortured me, but I loved him for it. Under another pile of stuff, I unearthed the scrapbook of clippings and inspirations for *George* that he had given me the first day we met. I read the index cards that were paper-clipped to different pages. "Washington Perspective: should not dominate the magazine" or "Media and Politics section: could be placed anywhere." I wondered whether I'd hit all of his marks.

Busying myself to quiet my racing mind, I wiped off the coffee table with Windex and threw away soda cans and potato chip bags. I organized my magazines, put film away, put my books back on the shelves, and sifted through papers, trying to put some order into a world that no longer made any sense. I threw away all the corporate memos, put bills in a separate pile, and filed cover sketches. As I sorted through yet another pile, a note on yellow lined notebook paper caught my attention: "Matt, let's not second-guess ourselves on this one, full speed ahead, JK." I stared at the note, admiring the familiar, jaunty handwriting.

In the days that followed, the phones stopped ringing, and the office became meaningless without John. I reached out to friends to help me get my mind off things. I called Jane Hsiang, and we went to Da Silvano. I was hoping to relive the day we had gone there with the first issue of *George* and tortured the other diners by not letting them see it. A well-known creative director minced into the restaurant wearing a bright red leather sport jacket with the sleeves pushed up, '80s style. "Aunt Jane, should I get a red leather jacket?" I asked, trying to trigger Aunt Jane. Aunt Jane looked over at the guy, and her beautiful cat eyes lit up. "Little Buddy, if I saw you wearing a red leather jacket like that, I'd be *very* concerned." Her comment and the delivery made me chuckle; it felt good to laugh with an old friend and find comfort knowing there were parts of my life that still remained good.

Rose and I leaned on each other. When she showed up at my apartment with a bag from Barneys containing three pairs of four-hundred-dollar Manolo Blahnik shoes that she couldn't afford, I asked her what she could have been thinking. She answered, "What was I *thinking*? I was thinking, *Everyone's dead and I want Manolos!*" We lived in a blur and did anything *not* to think about John or our futures. That summer, *Titanic* was playing every day on pay-per-view, and we watched it over and over like zombies. We'd chat and drink wine through the boring parts and quiet down for the parts we loved, like when Kate Winslet in the big hat turns and faces the camera, and when the *Titanic* begins to sink into the ocean and the giant propellers lift, dripping out of the water.

Every time Leo yelled, "I'm king of the world!" we'd shout in unison, "Lifetime achievement award!" because we *knew* that one day he'll be a little old man in a wheelchair and the Academy will play *that* scene. Watching the story about the loss of a great ship and a great love soothed us. The truth was, reality was here, and we were doing our best to hide from it.

10.

"OTHER THAN THAT, MRS. LINCOLN, HOW WAS THE PLAY?"

We were just going through the motions at the office. Each time we heard more bad news and another thread of hope was snatched away—like when the Coast Guard located John's plane underwater—my art director, Michelle, would look at me, I'd nod, and she'd press Play on a boom box to repeat "Concrete and Clay." The snappy one-hit wonder from the '60s began with a few clanks of a cowbell that comically emphasized how, absurdly, the tragic hits kept coming. It still makes me nostalgic when I hear those clanks and I'm transported back to those days.

On the morning of the memorial for John at the Church of St. Thomas More on the Upper East Side, the *George* staff met at Sarabeth's Kitchen. I'd never been to Sarabeth's because it was so far uptown and I'm more of a late-lunch type than a brunch type. No one had an appetite anyway. Christiane Amanpour soothed the group by telling stories about when she and John were housemates during their college days. I couldn't really pay attention; I was numb and felt like I was watching a movie or was in the middle of a dream. I could imagine telling a friend, "I had the weirdest dream that John died in a plane crash and Christiane Amanpour was having breakfast with us."

The walk over to the church remained dreamlike. I noticed that one of John's friends was working the front door. He was sort of a show-off. Even though it made me feel like an asshole, I couldn't help thinking that he was enjoying all the television coverage; the news cameras were aimed right at him. I walked in with Nancy Haberman, and we chose a pew. Nancy didn't have a lot of one-liners that day. No one did.

I'm the world's biggest rubbernecker when a celebrity walks into a restaurant, but I couldn't have cared less when Bill Clinton, Muhammad Ali, and Arnold Schwarzenegger arrived. I was nervous for RoseMarie, who read a beautiful poem. I relaxed a bit when she finished and sat down. When Wyclef Jean sang "Many Rivers to Cross," I thought, *Not in a goddamn plane, you asshole.* It was an inappropriate song choice. Numbness turned into anger then back into sadness, which seemed to be the pattern. Every heart in the room broke as Anthony Radziwill hobbled up to the altar to speak. John had been preoccupied with worry for the past year about Anthony's terminal illness, yet here was *Anthony* bidding farewell to *John*.

Ted Kennedy made an elegant speech ending with "We dared to think that this John Kennedy would live to comb gray hair." I chuckled to myself, remembering all the hair jokes John and I had made. I thought, *A receding hairline is better than a dead one,* and wished John had been there for me to rib.

After the emotionally draining service, there was a reception planned at some fancy old uptown mansion. As I quietly walked over with Nancy, I expected to hear my all-time favorite joke, which she says after something goes wrong: "Other than that, Mrs. Lincoln, how was the play?" It was *way* too close to home.

I entered the mansion and found Rose, and she reintroduced me to Carolyn's mother, Ann Freeman, and Carolyn's nana. It was impossible for me to imagine what they were feeling; they looked completely devastated. I told a silly story about Carolyn to them in what felt like slow motion. Ann took my hands and gently patted them, saying, "Oh, that sounds like her." I remembered that Carolyn had told me she smoked outside at her mom's house, freezing in the winter, because Ann hated the habit. I thought that Ann would wish that was her main problem today.

I lost Rose to a group of Carolyn's girlfriends and wandered off alone. I was feeling awkward around John and Carolyn's extended circle of friends. I found Biz Mitchell, *George*'s executive editor, standing by a window. In an effort to lighten things up, I looked down at her legs and said, "You still got 'em!" Biz and I shared a joke that "the legs were the last to go" and that she'd end up like Helen Gurley Brown, wearing short skirts until the end. We even joked that we would design a Lucite desk for her so visitors would always see those indestructible gams. I meandered around with my drink through the white marble halls and stairways, feeling like I didn't deserve to feel as sad as everyone else; they were much closer to John. I felt so disconnected that I couldn't wait to leave.

That night I invited the staff to my apartment to blow off some steam and be together. The apartment that I bought from Russell Simmons had come equipped with a state-of-the-art entertainment system that had huge speakers and a projection screen. I dimmed the lights and lit about sixty tea candles, which I placed on shelves, ledges, and windowsills. By the time everyone arrived, it looked like a mass at a medieval church. I loaded the CD player with a range of music: Caetano Veloso, the Beastie Boys, The Brothers Johnson, Paolo Conte, Fiona Apple, and Moby, and projected French Nouvelle Vague movies on the giant screen for atmosphere. Truffaut's *Day for Night* played with the sound off. I ordered a shitload of Thai food from my favorite hole-in-the-wall, East Village Thai, and had cases of red wine and beer from Astor Place Liquor sent over. It turned into a 5:00 a.m. blowout with people crashing on the sofa and chairs. I wished John could have been there.

A few days later, a memorial for Carolyn and her sister Lauren was held at Christ Church in the Bessettes' hometown of Greenwich, Connecticut. I'd driven past the church a million times on my way to the Greenwich Cinemas. It was an extremely hot Connecticut day like I remembered from my childhood, heavy and thick with humidity, and the church was not air-conditioned. I sat in a pew with RoseMarie and some of John's friends. Mourners' faces were red and swollen from the heat, men's collars were drenched, and we were sweating through our suits. I looked toward Pat Manocchia with my hands on my lapels and mimed removing my jacket. I mouthed the words *You chilly, want my jacket?* RoseMarie rolled her eyes at me. Half an hour later, the temperature had risen to the point where I was feeling faint. I leaned close to Rose and whispered, "You know what? I think it's more *hot* than *sad* here." That broke her up; her shoulders shook and she put her hands over her mouth. People probably thought she was sobbing. I can't remember the rest of that day; the heat had made an unbearable moment even weirder.

I was asked to speak at a memorial service for John to be held at the New-York Historical Society. This memorial was arranged for the professional community. What could I say to a room filled with New York, Hollywood, and Washington's elite? I decided to tell funny stories about John. I wasn't sure if that made sense for a eulogy, but it was the only way I knew to pay tribute. A day before the service, I jotted down several stories and went down to Marian McEvoy's office to bounce them off her. Marian was dressed in white linen, her collection of Victorian lava cameo bracelets clacking on her wrists. We sat at a round table in her office to work it through. She looked so chic and cool, even in the ninety-degree heat. Her nails were clean, cut and unpolished, which I loved. She read my ideas through her black reading glasses, which she proudly told everyone she got from Dr. Duane Reade. I don't think she needed them.

"Now, Matt-a-Rat, this is going to be great, but we have to practice." Marian circled stories that she felt were poignant and pushed the paper back to me. "Rat, type each of these ideas up on index cards and meet me at Le Taxi on East Sixtieth Street at eight thirty." As I walked out, Marian looked over her glasses at me, "Rat, eight thirty, don't be late."

At Le Taxi, Marian ordered seared scallops. I ordered a steak and fries and a bottle of wine, and we got down to business. She went through the cards, putting them in order: "This is a cute one, start with that." Fishing a Sharpie from her purse, she underlined words that should be emphasized, and then coached me on my delivery. "Don't forget to look around the room at different people." I cleared my throat and tried it out on her. "When John visited the art room—and by the way, he usually knocked on the door and shouted, 'Are you naked?'—" Marian stopped me. "Good, Rat! That's going to get a big laugh. So pause there, *and then* continue the story. Got it, Rat?" Marian was a natural entertainer and an expert at public speaking. She wouldn't send me up there unprepared.

The following day, I met Rose at Il Cantinori to try my speech out on her. I don't think Rose was expecting what I'd written, because after my first punch line, she did a spit take and sprayed her martini all over us. "Don't change one word, it's perfect."

"What time did you take the Valium?" Rose asked me at the memorial service. I shrugged, "I don't know; nine this morning, maybe?" "Take another now," she said, grabbing a glass of white wine from a passing tray, "and down this!" It was so hot, and I was anxious. The lobby was crowded, and I floated through it on my Valium and white wine high, greeting the people I knew. Sounds were either too soft or too loud, or someone seemed inches from my face or far away against a wall.

I glided farther into the room and ran into Barbara Cady, who said, "Remember to say Jean-Louis's first and last names when you mention him." I got the message. The second Valium took effect as I took my seat with the others. I watched as the auditorium filled with people. I saw Ben Stiller, Al Franken, Ann Coulter, and Howard Stringer, the head of Sony, settling in among the familiar faces from the Hachette offices.

George's executive editor, Richard Blow, gave a predictable speech. Jean-Louis gave a very dramatic speech that ended with something like "and now we are just left with memories." I remember thinking how *French* it was. I heard someone say my name, and I walked on stage. I spotted Ben Stiller up front and felt really uneasy. Would he think I wasn't funny? When I got to my first punch line there was an explosion of laughter; Marian and Rose had been right. I felt charged with energy as I went through each of my cards, which were basically the stories I tell in this book. I got to my last story, about having a huge argument with John at work. In the middle of the argument, I pleaded, "John, stop yelling at me!" John put his hands on my shoulders, smiled wide, and said, "Matt, we are *not* arguing! We're having a *passion-ate* conversation!" As the laughs died down, I ending by saying that knowing and working with John made us all stronger people and we would always be grateful.

I got a standing ovation. As I made my way back to my seat, Al Franken pointed his finger at me and said, "*That* was good." A jumping RoseMarie gave me her ultimate compliment: "You're a rock star!" Pat Manocchia, John's buddy, asked, "That was two Valiums and a glass of white wine?" I felt tranquilized by that combination but thought I had painted a good picture of what John was like. I was performing, like I had when John was alive, entertaining him with my jokes, hoping to make him laugh. I tried to convey the affection I felt for him through humor to avoid the sloppy sentimentality he would have hated and made fun of. Afterward in the lobby, Harold Evans, Tina Brown's husband, came up to me and said, "We all felt like he was *in* the room; you conjured him up."

The days after all of the memorials were inconsequential and empty. I hadn't really mourned in the normal way—no reflecting on the past, sobbing and hugging people. I made myself available to others when they needed to be consoled, but otherwise I kept to myself. One morning I threw my dirty shirts down the garbage chute in my building and arrived at the dry cleaner minutes later with a bag of trash.

Days later I left work feeling dizzy. I couldn't find a taxi, so I got on an R train heading downtown. By Twenty-third Street I was cold and sweaty, like I was going to pass out. As the train pulled into the Eighth Street station I watched the iron columns with 8s painted on them flicker past the window. I fought to stay conscious, but I awoke on the platform with a stranger looking down at me, saying, "Don't move, you're bleeding badly!" I'd hit one of those metal columns with my forehead when I'd collapsed. Trainloads of New Yorkers stepped *over* me. I must have looked like a drugged-up professional, lying on the cement in the blood-soaked Helmut Lang sport coat I had just gotten at Charivari on West Fifty-seventh Street.

It was embarrassing when the paramedics scooped me up and took me to Cabrini Medical Center. Nurses admitted me and hooked me up to an IV; I was severely dehydrated. I lay on a gurney wearing a drafty hospital gown and saw that my roommates were mostly homeless men brought in from the streets. A nurse brought me a telephone with a long cord so I could call a friend or family member. I stared at the ceiling with the phone on my stomach, wondering if I should call my mom. She'd just freak out, and I didn't want her to come all the way into the city. I decided not to call anyone. I rarely feel alone; it's a survival tactic left over from my childhood. What could anyone do besides wait? And I didn't want anyone to see me in a hospital gown with my ass exposed. I listened to doctors and nurses discuss how many stitches I should have and whether they could locate a plastic surgeon. I'd given myself another scar.

Hachette decided to continue producing *George* with a new editor. He was the furthest thing from John possible, with zero charm. I sorted out a severance package with Hachette and was out of there, unsure of what my next move might be.

In the following months, being the orphaned creative director of *George* magazine made me the hottest commodity in the magazine world. Calls poured in with invitations to meet New York's top editors, but all I could do was stay home and watch *The Sopranos* and reruns of *Who's the Boss?* The answering machine was always on, screening. I lived in an airtight world, deciding who I would call back, when I would go out, and, most important, what to eat for dinner.

I knew I needed to find work, but I was paralyzed with self-doubt. I was depressed, and nothing mattered after my unimaginable life had changed so dramatically. Maybe I was a mediocre art director and John just *liked* me? Was it possible that John kept me around because he thought I was funny? Each time a new magazine position was offered, I found a good reason why I couldn't accept it. *Elle* Italia flew me to Milan for a noon meeting and didn't offer me lunch. What kind of Italians *were* they? *Asia Week* in Hong Kong was too far away. I nixed Germany's *Amica* magazine after I decided it was too close to Dachau.

It didn't matter what the job was, where it was, or how much money I was offered; nothing could be like *George.* I was like the kid who lost his dad and couldn't bear to see his mother go on a date. I felt exposed without John, who was always able to sense my uneasiness from a glance or a gesture, and always had a solution. If I fumbled while presenting ideas to magazine executives, John knew just what to interject to put me back on track. When I felt intimidated by the Hollywood star we were shooting for a cover, John eased my fears. "Matt, she's a really *ordinary, uneducated* person, but with a *lot* of money. Don't be scared."

Once, I was scheduled to have breakfast with Tina Brown to discuss her magazine, *Talk,* but canceled at the last minute, making up some bullshit excuse. I felt like a jerk. The truth was that I was afraid I would disappoint her and everyone else who called; with John gone, I had lost my hard-won confidence.

I spent a childhood of doing anything I could do not to be noticed, but somehow John had the ability to *see* me. The fact that he valued our collaboration and friendship helped me feel like a complete person. In just a few years, John made his way into my psyche with that kind of force.

It's amazing to think that I never received an email from John. We didn't use it yet at *George*; we used telephones, FedEx, and fax machines. I wonder what John would think about an iPhone or Facebook, and then I realize he didn't even live to see the tsunami in Phuket or the horrors of September 11, only blocks from his home.

Everyone on television eulogized John as if they knew him. Those who never met him have written articles and books. Every network aired *The True Story* or *A Tribute*. They were all capitalizing on his death, cashing in. Everyone had something to say, but they all missed the point. John was a real person—not only the son of Camelot but also a funny, passionate, inspiring, yet unassuming regular guy. John brought out the best in everyone and saw potential in people when they didn't see it in themselves. He was the guy who, when approached by A&E for their *Biography* series, thought they were crazy and said, "Tell them I'm *way* too young to do a biography. Wait till I'm dead."

I thought about what Harold Evans said after my speech at John's memorial: "You conjured him up; we could all *feel* him in the room." I don't believe in ghosts, but I think that when you love and admire someone very much, they live on inside you.

A couple of years ago, I was in the car with my cousin Gary and his wife, Alison, and we were mimicking our grandmother. With any subject that arose, either Gary or I would bellow the comment Grandma would have made. "Where should we eat?" Alison asked. "Look, who the hell knows? Matthew didn't bring a sport jacket, and that limits our choices," Gary answered in Grandma's exact rhythm and tone. Alison laughed as I added, "You can't just *waltz* into Charley's Crab in the height of the season with no reservation!" "You guys are actually scaring me now," Alison said, irritated. I think those voices are the ghosts, and rarely a day passes when we don't hear them haunting and guiding us.

I hear John's voice guiding me when I find myself in need of advice, *What would John have done? What would John say?* John is gone, and I feel an even stronger connection to him. John used to say that privileged people who never faced any challenges, people who went through life without trauma, were clueless, and that made them the hardest for the rest of us to deal with. Some people remain untested, unmarked by life because they've never been touched by death. I was obsessed about my imperfections, and John taught me that it was the flaws that made people *real*.

John never looked at my scars, he never once asked what happened. The thing that I thought alienated me he didn't even notice—he concentrated on my essence. The world was attracted to John's perfect persona and seemed to ignore his essence. John saw past flaws and had the ability to see people regardless of how they presented themselves or were seen by others. He taught me that my flaws *allowed* me to develop gifts that helped me to live in a world that was far from perfect.

Once, John breezed past my office door while I was in the middle of one of my rants with Rose. "It was a Friday," was the last part of the sentence he heard. He stopped and swung into the room. "Friday, what was a Friday?" "The day God created you," I answered. "You know, it was the end of a long week, God was feeling good, wanted to get going for the weekend, and he said, 'Give him everything.'"

John clapped his hands together and laughed. "Rosie, is he talking about my hairline again?" he asked, certain that I must have been going on about his immunity to male-pattern baldness. I continued, "It's like all of God's assistants were running into his office asking, 'Boss, should we give him super thick hair? Should his father be a butcher in Greenpoint or the president of the United States? Five foot three or six foot one? Tan skin? Muscular?'" John roared. I stood up from the sofa and moved closer to him. "So God signed off on everything in your favor; six foot one tall, great body, fancy-schmantzy family." John cried out, "You're psychotic!" I kept going, "'Boss, twenty-twenty vision, right?'" As usual, John walked out of my office with his hands over his face, shaking his head.

It always *did* seem like John had everything. What I realized was, with him in my life, so did I.

ACKNOWLEDGMENTS

To my agent, Steve Troha, and to my editor, Tricia Boczkowski, and her team at Simon & Schuster; Louise Burke, Jen Bergstrom, Jen Robinson, Emilia Pisani, and Elana Cohen: thanks for turning my dinner-table tales into a real book.

RoseMarie Terenzio; I know this is boring, call me later; your support through the years is never taken for granted. It's been the best ride to hell in a handbasket (and back) anyone could hope for.

My cousin, Seth Plotnick, my partner in crime from childhood to today, your wisdom over the years and help on this book is immeasurable.

A special thank you to: Molly Dowd, Laura Forde, Matt Gorrek, Claudine Ingeneri, Missy Rayder, Margaret Russell, Melissa Seley, and Gregory Woo. Your constant enthusiasm for this book kept me moving ahead.

ACKNOWLEDGMENTS

Thank you to those who listened patiently, dug up photos, or offered encouragement over the past couple of years: Platon Antoniou, Christine Aure, Laurence Benaïm, Mary Brogger, Marina Burini, Alex Cayley, Jake Chessum, Sean Daly, Dave DeMattei, Arione de Winter, Jacqueline Goewey, Fred Goisbault, Stanley Goldstein, Annabelle Grusq, Sally Hamilton, Fred Jacobs, Joy Lockerby, Brian Lotti, Laura Lotti, Courtney Lynch, Rita Marmor, Ned Martel, Toby McFarlan Pond, Ralph Merola, Andy Nguyen, Kyle Pope, Jorge Roman-Zeno, Thomas Schenk, Michele Schiavone, Jeffrey Seroy, Alexander Shannon, Mario Sorrenti, Michelle Tessler, Nikki Thean, Ken Tokunaga, Marko Velk, Patrick Wade, Melanie Ward, and Ben Wiseman.

Carolyn Bessette Kennedy, Barbara Cady, Jean-Louis Ginibre, John F. Kennedy Jr., and Carl Robbins: I miss you all, and you bring a smile to my face each time I think of you.

PHOTOGRAPHY CREDITS

Insert 1. **Page 1:** Reuters/Corbis (*top*); Stanley Goldstein (*bottom*). **Page 2:** Courtesy of the author (*top, middle right, bottom right, bottom left*); Mario Sorrenti (*middle left*). **Page 3:** Matt Berman (*top left*); courtesy of the author (*bottom left*); Alberto Vargas (*top right*); Herb Ritts (*bottom left*) large image. **Page 4:** Matt Berman (*top left*); *George* magazine cover, July 1997, photograph by Stéphane Sednaoui (*top right*); *George* magazine cover, December 1995, photograph by Nick Knight (*middle left*); *George* magazine cover, January 1997, photograph by Satoshi Saïkusa (*middle right*); *George* magazine cover, September 1997 (*bottom right*) and September 1996 (*bottom left*), photographs by Mario Sorrenti. **Page 5:** George Tames/Smithsonian Institution (*top right*); Matt Berman (*top left*); *George* magazine spreads, December 1998, photographs by Ellen

PHOTOGRAPHY CREDITS

von Unwerth (*middle* and *bottom*). **Page 6:** Courtesy of the author. **Page 7:** Courtesy of the author. **Page 8:** L. Busacca/Getty Images.

Insert 2. Page 1: Polaroids courtesy of the author; Jake Chessum (*bottom left*). **Pages 2–3:** Polaroids courtesy of the author; *George* magazine cover, August 1997, photograph by Stéphane Sednaoui (*bottom left*). **Page 4:** Bev Parker (*top left*); courtesy of the author (*top right*); Platon (*middle left*); courtesy of the author (*middle right*); Ellen von Unwerth (*bottom right*); *George* magazine cover, September 1998, photograph by Satoshi Saïkusa (*bottom left*). **Page 5:** Courtesy of the author (*top*); Michael Thompson (*middle row*); courtesy of the author (*bottom*). **Page 6:** Stephane Cardinale/Sygma/Corbis (*top left*); Matt Berman (*top right*); courtesy of the author (*bottom*). **Page 7:** Matt Berman (*top left*); Barry Blitt/*Vanity Fair* (*top right*); courtesy of the author (*bottom right, middle left, bottom left*). **Page 8:** Courtesy of the author (*top left*), *George* magazine cover, October 1999, photograph by Nathaniel Goldberg/Hachette.

208

GEORGE MAGAZINE COVER CHRONOLOGY

1995

1. Cindy Crawford

1996

2. Robert De Niro
3. Charles Barkley
4. Howard Stern
5. Demi Moore
6. Newt Gingrich
7. Drew Barrymore
8. Richard Nixon (historical)
9. Barbra Streisand
10. Woody Harrelson

COVER CHRONOLOGY

1997

11. Claudia Schiffer
12. Karen Mulder
13. Julia Roberts
14. Wegman dog
15. Katie Couric
16. George Clooney
17. Jenny McCarthy
18. Harrison Ford
19. Kate Moss
20. Elizabeth Hurley
21. Barbara Walters
22. Kevin Costner

1998

23. Pamela Anderson
24. Robert De Niro and Dustin Hoffman
25. John Travolta
26. Tom Hanks
27. Christy Turlington
28. Johnny Depp
29. Bruce Willis
30. Charlize Theron
31. The Spirit of '76 (models)
32. Edward Norton
33. Peter Jennings
34. Sean Penn

COVER CHRONOLOGY

1999

35. Robert Duvall
36. Ronald Reagan (historical)
37. Elizabeth Hurley and Matthew McConaughey
38. Garth Brooks
39. Calista Flockhart
40. Liam Neeson
41. Salma Hayek
42. Ben Stiller
43. Rob Lowe
44. JFK Jr. memorial issue